The Irish Line

Farmers, Industrialists, Doctors, Soldiers, Missionaries, Administrators and Family Men.

ORIGIN OF THE GRIMSHAW IRISH LINE

Walter de Grimshaw c. 1250

Henry de Grimshaw c. 1283

Adam de Grimshaw c. 1313

Henry Grimshaw c. 1317

Adam Grimshaw = Cicely de Clayton c. 1342

Henry de Grimshaw c. 1372

Robert Grimshaw c. 1424

Henry Grimshaw c. 1442

Nicholas Grimshaw c. 1481

George Grimshaw c. 1551

Nicholas Grimshaw c. 1593 Head of Pendle Forest Line

Thomas Grimshaw of Heyhouses c. 1622

Nicholas Grimshaw of Heyhouses d 1651

Nicholas Grimshaw of Heyhouses 1636 -1708

Nicholas Grimshaw of Padiham d. 1736 = Anne Grimshaw

Nicholas Grimshaw of Blackburn b 1714 = Susan Briercliffe

Nicholas Grimshaw of Blackburn b 1747 = Mary Longley

THE GRIMSHAW IRISH LINE

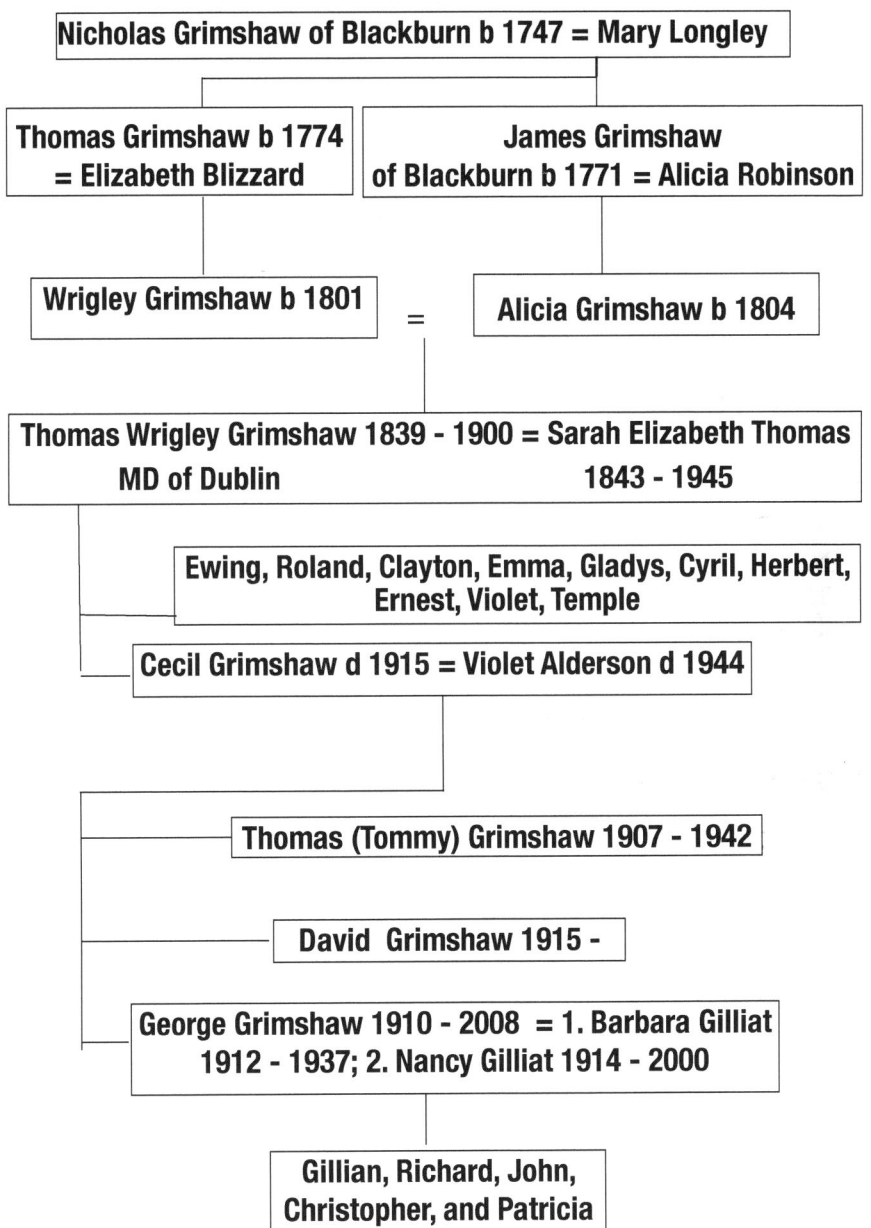

ACKNOWLEDGEMENTS

In writing this chronicle I decided to thread together what others have written before. I have added a little in order to make the threads work better. The early family history comes from Tom Grimshaw's (no direct relative who lives in Texas) extensive website "Grimshaw Family Origins" to which George Grimshaw, Hilary Tulloch and I have all contributed to. Thank you Tom. Cecil Grimshaw's adventures are from his diary and from Boer War and Gallipoli reports that are available on the Internet. David Grimshaw (George Grimshaw's younger brother, and at the time of writing still alive and living in Australia) wrote most about their life after the First World War at Grattons (The Legacy). Nancy Grimshaw is such a good writer, so that the piece about her childhood is her own. Most of the rest are from recordings that George made to Gill (daughter) and Harry Foot, and youngest daughter Patsy Fostiropoulos, when he was over 90 - good memory!

Photo credits go to David Grimshaw, John Grimshaw, Patsy Fostiropoulos, and the family archives.

The balance and that is not much, can be attributed to me, the scribe!

Thank you all, and as they say nowadays - enjoy!

Richard Grimshaw - December 2011

The Irish Line

Farmers, Industrialists, Doctors, Soldiers, Missionaries, Administrators and Family Men

Introduction

This is the story of a line of Grimshaws that can be traced back for 800 years. It starts with Walter de Grimshaw who lived and farmed near Blackburn in Lancashire and ends with George Grimshaw who eventually settled down in Ringmore, Devon and died there in 2008 in his 98th year. A fair bit of the text is verbatim - copy of pieces written by the individual Grimshaws themselves or by others who have been interested in their exploits. I make no apology as I can hardly improve on the original. The text is backed by old and modern photographs and images. This is an account about ordinary but privileged English men and women who in the main put their country and fellow men and women first, both in peace and war. They lived interesting, but not extraordinary lives. They were first and foremost family men and women (including those that they chose to marry), and the majority were professionals in the civil or military services. They cared greatly for their country and their fellow citizens. The seven generations of Grimshaws whom appear in this book, as individuals, were part of, and contributed to the huge industrial and social changes that changed the world over the past 250 years. The account of their lives is written for the future generations of this line of Grimshaws (known as the Irish line) so that they might know a little more of their rich heritage, and be proud of it.

Grimshaw - A family with a Lancashire heritage

The Grimshaws have origins in Lancashire traceable to around 1000 A.D. with probable connection to the town of Grimsargh, northeast of Preston. There are few records of Grimshaw family lines for the first 200 to 250 years. The earliest was Walter de Grimshaw about 1250 A.D. who lived about three miles southeast Blackburn.

The location of Walter de Grimshaw is on a stream called

Grimshaw country - Eccleshill and Ooze Castle Wood

Grimshaw Brook and forms the boundary between two ancient, small townships – Eccleshill to the west, and Yate and Pickup Bank to the east. Grimshaw is located on the west side of the stream just inside Eccleshill. The Grimshaw location was greatly affected by development during the Industrial Revolution.

The Grimshaw family retained their land holdings in Eccleshill even after they relocated to Clayton-le-Moors in the mid 1300s. A Grimshaw living at Clayton Hall whilst traveling to the family's holdings in Eccleshill performed a valuable community service by killing a large snake in Ooze Castle Wood, about a mile southeast of the Grimshaw location.

The snake-killing event, perhaps at least partly a legend, would have happened between 1350, when the Grimshaws moved to Clayton Hall, and 1613, when the arms were sanctioned by the Kings' herald. Thus the Griffin preceded the snake in

Grimshaw history by at least 300 years.

Although Walter de Grimshaw of Eccleshill is the progenitor of the earliest recorded Grimshaw family, the family was in existence for up to 300 years before 1250, when Walter was born. Many researchers believe that "Grimshaw" is derived from, or has a common origin with, the community of "Grimsargh", which is located northeast of Preston. The earliest recorded Grimshaw family lived at the Grimshaw location in Eccleshill until the mid 1300s. The Grimshaw family then relocated to Clayton Hall, in Clayton-le-Moors northeast of Blackburn, because of a fortuitous marriage into the Clayton family. The family lived at Clayton-le-Moors for many generations until the heirs ran out in about 1715 and the estate passed to the Lomax family.

There are two competing theories of the original derivation of the Grimshaw name. The earlier Celtic derivation is based on the hypothesis that the terms "grim" and "grin" are forms of the one root word (that) signify the sun, when the term is used for that celestial luminary as a divinity, or as the object or symbol referred to in divine worship. These terms were Angle and Saxon terms when they occupied the lowlands that they had seized from the Celts. If this theory is true, then most likely the very original Grimshaw location is west of Pendle Hill, perhaps not far from Grimsargh.

The later Viking derivation is based on the hypothesis that Grimshaw refers to "Grim'rs wood", where the Grimr, a recurrent personal name in Viking place-names, had ambivalent overtones. Sometimes it seems to have signified the god Odin, thought to go about disguised in a grim mask. At other times it seems to stand as a nickname for the devil.

One of the most important Grimshaw lines to originate from the original Grimshaw family tree was the "Pendle Forest" line, which was located at Heyhouses on Pendle Hill and in the area on the east side of the hill. The connection of the Pendle Forest line to the more senior Eccleshill and Clayton-le-Moors

Grimshaw line (as published in Thomas D. Whitaker's History of Whalley, 1875) has now been established, thanks to the work of W.J. Abram *(articles in the Preston Guardian, 1877) and Farrer and Brownbill (Victoria County History of Lancashire, volume 6, "Filly Close", published 1911).*

Two Grimshaw brothers: left, James (1771 to 1865) and right, Thomas (1774 to 1855):

Alicia (1804 to 1847) daughter of James married Wrigley (1801 to 1878) son of Thomas.

Grimshaw – The Irish Line

The Irish line of Grimshaws came about when Nicholas Grimshaw migrated to northern Ireland from Lancashire in 1760. Nicholas brought with him his father, Nicholas, who died in 1775. His two eldest sons, James and Thomas were the line's progenitors. James daughter Alicia married her cousin Wrigley, the latter was Thomas' son. This bit of inbreeding doesn't appear to have harmed future generations!

Nicholas' son William wrote the following account about his father, it is particularly of interest since it is part of the early industrial revolution coming to Ireland.

"My father, the late Nicholas Grimshaw, being the first that introduced the spinning of cotton twist into Ireland, besides being a person of liberal education, and great public spirit, seems to have been a leading character, in his neighbourhood, from nearly his earliest settlement in the country. He was a native of Blackburn, in Lancashire, the birth-place of the late Sir Robert Peel (the latter was the father of Sir Robert Peel, Prime Minister of England who among other things established the metropolitan police in London); who, I have understood, was a near relation of my father's; and I know we have, in our family, the same Christian names as the Peels, viz. Thomas, Edmund, William, and Robert. My father and Mr. Peel were nearly of the same age, and commenced business about the same time; but they were of very different dispositions; the former being fond of improving his property, by the planting of trees, and other ornaments, and also passing his summers at the fashionable watering-places in England; incurring an expense, not altogether warranted in a manufacturer, having fourteen children to support. He was also unremittingly attentive to the interests of the public; to which, Mr. Peel, being a man of much less education than my father was, in the early part of his career, but very slightly devoted.

The late Nicholas Grimshaw, who filled the office of mayor of the city of Preston, for more than forty consecutive years; and

Alicia wife of James Grimshaw and mother of Alicia Wrigley Grimshaw.

also the late Henry Fielding, of Garstang; were first cousins of my father's. Our name is pure Anglo-Saxon, signifying "a dark wood;" and there is a dilapidated village, in Lancashire, where in ancient times was the residence of our family, from which it is derived.

My father came to Ireland, as I can collect from the births registered in the family Bible, about the year 1760, shortly after the improved system of spinning cotton-twist, the invention of which seems, with justice, partly to be attributed to Richard (afterwards Sir Richard) Arkwright, had been brought to some degree of efficiency, if not of perfection. His motive for settling in Ireland seems to have been two-fold, - first to evade the operation of Arkwright's patent, (which did not, at any time, extend to Ireland,) and secondly, to reap advantage from the comparatively low rate of wages in that country. But in both these objects, he had evidently miscalculated. The advantage derived from the non-payment for the patent-right, was more than counterbalanced by the isolated position in which he placed himself, with regard to the obtaining of machinery, and the speedy adoption of new improvements; and the difference of wages was equally countervailed, by the waste and expense attending the instruction and training of raw hands. The consequence was, that, although the profits were considerable, owing to the infancy of the business, and the small competition, yet, in the course of time, he found himself constrained to apply to the Irish Parliament, for protection, in the nature of what is now called a tariff, amounting to ten per cent, upon cotton-twist; and, subsequently, when he commenced the printing of calicoes, in which he became highly distinguished for his taste and the permanency of his colours, he induced the parliament to impose a protective duty, also, on the latter article, amounting to more than one shilling per square yard; duties, which, it will appear, in the sequel, con-

Above The Whitehouse garden and view of Cave Hill, and below Whitehouse, County Antrim, near Belfast, Ireland arounf 1850.

tributed rather to retard, than to accelerate the extension and perfection of the cotton manufacture, in Ireland.

My father's first place of settlement was in the parish of Belfast, county of Antrim, about three miles north of that town, and five from the ancient, but poverty-stricken city, of Carrickfergus, on the site of an old linen bleach-green, or flax-mill, called Greencastle; where the writer of this memoir was born. In a small building, still in existence, near the high-road, and the sea-shore, at a landing-place, known as the Lime-stones, was erected the first machinery for spinning cotton-twist in Ireland. The machine being circular, and kept in motion both day and night, realized, in the first year, the enormous sum of eighteen hundred pounds. The water, however, at Greencastle, being found insufficient for an extensive business, my father purchased another site, adjoining, and further to the north, situated in the parish of Carnmoney; upon which, is since erected the beautiful and extensive village of Whitehouse, still the property of my family, with more than three hundred dwelling-houses, and having appurtenant one hundred and seventy English acres of good land, surrounded by a plantation of trees, with other rural improvements; in which, my brothers take great delight.

At Whitehouse, in conjunction with Mr. Nathaniel Wilson, a gentleman of some enterprise and capital, a new cotton-mill was erected, in 1785, capable of holding four thousand spindles and preparation; and, about ten years afterwards, by the enlargement of an old building, originally used for bleaching lawns, by a lady, named Tomb, another mill was organized, containing about an equal number of spindles; which was the greatest extent ever ventured on by any of the family; and these two mills, about twelve years ago, were converted to the purpose of spinning flax; the spinning of cotton in Ireland, having become almost wholly unprofitable, owing to the gigantic competition in Great Britain.

Belfast, which, at the time my father settled in its neighbourhood, contained only about ten thousand inhabitants, now reckons, at both sides of the Lagan, in the counties of Antrim and Down, not less than one hundred thousand."

Clarke (1938) provides additional historical information on the early development of the textile industry in Ireland:

"...The linen trade also suffered in the closing years of the century from the competition of the cotton trade. The rise of this industry is closely associated with our parish and is connected with the name of Nicholas Grimshaw, who established the first mill for spinning cotton twist at Whitehouse. "To the practical knowledge, genius and industry of this gentleman this country stands very highly indebted (Dubourdieu)

Grimshaw came to Whitehouse from Lancashire about 1760. He was accompanied by his father, also Nicholas Grimshaw, who was buried in our churchyard in 1775. The older Grimshaw was apparently interested in linen for in 1762, Magee printed a book for him on bleaching. His son, "the father of the cotton trade" was probably a man of small capital and his first venture at spinning was taken at the Belfast Poor House. Here Henry Joy and Thomas McCabe had a cotton spinning machine made at their own expense under Grimshaw's direction in 1777. The main motive of the undertaking was to give employment to the children in the Institution, and for some years the young people produced gloves, stockings and other articles. In 1784 Grimshaw, in partnership with Nathaniel Wilson, built at Whitehouse the first Irish mill for spinning twist by water-power, and the cotton industry was soon firmly established in Co. Antrim. The firm also specialized in calico printing and was noted for the style and elegance of its goods. In 1800 Grimshaw estimated that the cotton industry was giving employment to 13,000 people, and indirect employment to 14,000 others within a distance of twelve miles of Belfast.

Grimshaw acquired the townland of Ballygolan from the Marquess of Donegall together with the water rights in the Glasna-Braddon. He lived at Longwood and built several houses for his sons: -- Glas-na-Braddon, Ballygolan Lodge and Frogmore. He also planted the Long Wood and built much of Upper Whitehouse.

He had seven sons and two daughters, most of whom remained in the district and engaged in linen and cotton manufacture. It is said that on the usual Bank holiday fete on the Cave Hill in 1840 no less than forty Grimshaws were present. This "Ulster Father" died in 1895 and was buried in our churchyard."

Boyle (1839, p. 51) provides additional insight into the influence of the Grimshaws on the introduction and development of cotton textiles in Ireland:

Dr. and Mrs Thomas Felix Thomas, parents of Sarah Elizabeth Thomas who married Thomas Wrigley Grimshaw

"In 1786 the first cotton manufactory in Ireland was established in the adjoining parish of Shankill and on the verge of this parish, by the late Nicholas Grimshaw Esquire, who had previously come from England and settled in this parish. He soon after established the very extensive cotton printing and spinning manufactories which had until the year 1834 been carried on by his sons, and was the first to establish in this country a trade in which so much capital from this county has been embarked. The introduction of the cotton trade into Carnmoney laid the foundation of the great improvement which it has since undergone. The extensive employment the manufactories afforded not merely occupies the few unemployed labouring people in this, but attracted numbers from the surrounding parishes to such a degree that the populous villages of Whitehouse Upper and Whiteabbey are to them indebted for their origin and erection. The wages then given to printers and others were most liberal. The consumption of provisions and farm produce was of course materially increased, capital was more freely circulated in the parish and a stimulus was given to agriculture in consequence of the increased consumption of farm produce. Several other manufactories were established soon after in the parish, but of these there is now but one engaged in the printing business.

Dr. Thomas Wrigley Grimshaw of Dublin

Thomas Wrigley Grimshaw, son of Wrigley and Alicia Grimshaw and great grandson of Nicholas Grimshaw, was born in Whitehouse, County Antrim, in 1839, and learned his medicine at the Dublin School of Medicine when its reputation was at its highest.

If his teachers strayed from the art of bedside medicine into science it was into meteorology that had been revived by

Thomas Wrigley Grimshaw (1839 to 1900) married Sarah Elizabeth Thomas (1843 to 1945)

Thomas Sydenham, the 'English Hippocrates' in the seventeenth century. When Thomas was appointed Registrar Gen-

Thomas Wrigley and Sarah Grimshaw and family, from left to right: Cyril, Ernest, Emma, Roland, Clayton, Cecil, Thomas, Gladys, Herbert and Ewing

eral for Ireland in 1879 he diverted attention from the acute epidemics of zymotic diseases to chronic pulmonary affections that numerically were far more deadly. Cartography became an obsession with him, and he used it to show that Ireland was divided by phthisis (wasting diseases like tuberculosis into east and west. Koch's 'great discovery' in 1882 that tuberculosis is an infection not a 'constitutional' disease made him change his long-held views, and in the decade before his death in 1900 at Carrickmines, County Dublin, he became an active advocate of the new knowledge, distressed by the fact that thriving Belfast and its hinterland had the highest mortality from phthisis in Ireland. His concern for the health of young girls employed in large numbers in the linen factories was matched by his landmark advocacy of young ladies anxious to gain the licence to practise medicine in Great Britain and Ireland."

Thomas married Sarah Elizabeth Thomas on 11th April 1865. Thomas died on January 27th 1900 at the age of 60. Sarah went on to live until she was over 101 dying on April 29th 1945 in Essex. They had twelve children: Ewing b, 1876, Indian Army – Punjabis; Ernest b, 1870, Royal Navy; Herbert b, 1974 Judge; Cecil b, 1875, Royal Dublin Fusiliers; Cyril b, 1877, Assam tea planter; Roland b, 1880, Indian Army; Emma b,1882, Red Cross nurse; Gladys b, 1883; and Clayton b, 1885, Royal Navy.

The family due to its Belfast origins made numerous visits to relatives and family members in the northern part of the country. There were twelve children in Thomas Wrigley's family, of which three died young. A well developed nose and a broad backward turning thumb seem to have been a family characteristic amongst the men. It is not known whether they had more than their share of family pride but it is said that they were easily recognized "as having the Devil's own pride and bloody big noses"! or so the story goes.

Be that as it may, all the family served their country well in their various capacities. Ewing joined the Indian Army and commanded the 111 Punjab Regiment, as did his son Major General Harry Grimshaw (see Who's Who 1989) after him. Ewing was killed in action in the first World War. Ernest served in the Navy and later became a solicitor. Cyril was a tea planter and also served in the Assam Light Horse. Herbert became a Judge in Cyprus. Roly was in the Poona Horse and was severely gassed in World War 1. He died prematurely as a result in the mid 1930's. Cecil was killed in the Cape Hellas landing

Dr. Thomas wrigley Grimshaw (standing right) makes a presentation at the Duchess of Marlborough's Famine Relief Committee

on Gallipoli in April 1915; Clayton was also in the Navy. Emma was decorated by the Red Cross for her nursing services, and Gladys married Con Alexander, who falsified his age to join up in the first World War when he was too young, and again in the second World War when he was too old! Little wonder perhaps that Granny Grimshaw who died at the age of 101 in 1945 survived all of them except Cyril.

A Chronical of Thomas Wrigley Grimshaw's Life by J.W. Moore is in the following obituary.

"With pained surprise Dublin learned on the morning of January 23 the melancholy tidings of the unexpected and almost sudden death of this able member of the medical profession. Dr. Grimshaw succumbed on the 7th day to an attack of post-influenzal bronchopneumonia, in the sixty-first year of his age.

Thomas Wrigley Grimshaw was born on November 16, 1839, at Whitehouse, Go. Antrim. He was descended from the Grimshaws of Whalley, Lancashire, his great-grandfather having migrated from that place to Greencastle, Co. Antrim, where he founded the calico-printing industry in Ireland. Dr. Grimshaw's father was Wrigley Grimshaw, F.R.C.S.I., an eminent dentist, who was dental Surgeon to Stevens' Hospital, Mercer's Hospital, and the Pitt Street Institution for Diseases of Children.

The subject of this memoir was educated at Bryce's Academy; at Carrickfergus School; at the Academic Institute, Harcourt-street, Dublin; and at the Dublin High School, St. Stephen's-green, Dublin, under the ferule of Matthias Hare, LL.D. He graduated in Arts in the University of Dublin in 1860, obtaining first Junior Moderatorship in Experimental and Natural Science at the Degree Examination in Michaelmas Term of that year. At this time Grimshaw was busy with his professional studies in the School of Physic in Ireland, Sir Patrick Dun's Hospital, and Steevens' Hospital, and on June 26, 1861, he took the degrees of M.B. and M.Ch. in the University of Dublin. In 1862 he was enrolled as a Licentiate of the Royal College of Surgeons in Ireland. His further professional qualifications were – M.D. Univ. Dubl., 1867; Licentiate of the Royal College of Physicians of Ireland (1867), Fellow (1869), Diplomate in State Medicine, Trinity College, Dublin (1874). In recognition of his brilliant answering for the last-named qualification

Dr. Thomas Wrigley Grimshaw CB, MD. Registrar of Ireland (1839 - 1900)

the degree of Master of Arts was conferred upon him stipendiis condonatis. From the outset of his professional career, Grimshaw threw himself into the active practice of his calling as a physician with marvelous energy. For several years he was one of the physicians to Steevens' Hospital, filling in the Medical School formerly attached to that institution the lectureships in succession on Botany, Materia Medica, and Medicine. He served for fourteen years as visiting Physician to Cork Street Fever Hospital and wrote a number of medical reports on the work done in the hospital, which are of the highest statistical and scientific value. He acted also as Physician to the Coombe Lying-in Hospital, as Examiner in Practice of Medicine and Materia, Medica, in the Queen's University of Ireland, as Censor and Examiner in Medicine in the Royal College of Physicians of Ireland, and as Examiner in Vital Statistics in the University of Dublin.

In the autumn of 1879 Dr. Grimshaw was appointed Registrar-General for Ireland in succession to Dr. William Malachi Burke, who had died of an attack of pleuropneumonia on August 13 in that year. This necessitated his retirement from practice; but the renown he had achieved for himself found expression in his appointment as Honorary Consulting Physician to both Steevens' Hospital and Cork-street Fever Hospital, as well as to the Dublin Orthopedic Hospital.

As Registrar-General, Dr. Grimshaw devoted all his great energies during more than twenty years to the service of his country and to the welfare of its people. He died absolutely in harness, for within six days of his death, with his fatal malady upon him, he was in his office at Charlemont House, Dublin.

Dr. Grimshaw received many marks of public esteem as the years went by. He was President of the Statistical Society of Ireland in 1888-1890, of the Dublin Sanitary Association from 1885 to 1888, and, above all, of the Royal College of Physicians of Ireland in 1895 and 1896. He was a member of the Commission on the Dietary of Irish Prisons in 1880, and of the Commission to inquire into the sanitary condition of the Royal Barracks, Dublin, in 1887. He was author of many important papers on medicine, fever, sanitary and statistical questions. In conjunction with the writer of this memoir, he published in 1875 a paper on an infective form of pneumonia, which the authors termed "pythogenic pneumonia," and so foreshadowed the modern doctrine of the aetiology of pneumonia. He was joint author of the "Manual of Public Health for Ireland," published shortly after the passing of the "Public Health (Ireland) Act, 1875." The pages of this Journal have been enriched from time to time by many valuable papers from his pen. His Governmental Reports are models of their kind. They extend over twenty years, and deal with births, deaths, and marriages in Ireland, agriculture, emigration, crime, judicial statistics, banking and railway statistics. It fell to his lot to superintend the Census of 1881 and the Census of 1891, and at the time of his too early death the arrangements for taking the Census of 1901 had been almost completed by him. In 1897, the year of the Queen's "Diamond Jubilee," he received the well-won distinction of a Companionship of the Bath.

In private life Dr. Grimshaw showed an attractive personality. At the early age of 26 he married, on April 11, 1865, Sarah Elizabeth (Settie), daughter of the late Rev. Thomas Felix Thomas, of Broadlands, Newport, Isle of Wight. By her he had twelve children, of which nine survive him – seven sons and two daughters. His eldest son, Temple, died of "croup" (diphtheria) on October 18, 1872, aged 6-1/2 years; his eldest daughter, Violet Settie, died of scarlatina May 5, 1874, aged nearly 5 years. These, and the death of his daughter-in-law in 1898, were the great sorrows of his marriage, which was otherwise one of much happiness and content. Five of his sons have already reached manhood. Three of them are "Soldiers of the Queen," all having served or serving at present in the Royal Dublin Fusiliers. One of these officers, Lieutenant Cecil Thomas Grimshaw is now a prisoner of war at Pretoria. His eldest surviving son, Ewing Wrigley Grimshaw, of the Indian Staff Corps, married in 1893 the daughter of Lieut. Col. W. R. Kaye, of the Army Pay Department. This lady unfortunately died in 1898, leaving two little girls, who have been living with their grandparents at Priorsland, Carrickmine, Co. Dublin.

Dr. Grimshaw was a philanthropist of transparent sincerity. His life-work and his pleasure were to benefit his fellow-creatures, to improve the lot of the less fortunate among them, and to relieve them in sickness and sorrow. His loss to the Dublin Hospital Sunday Fund, to the National Association for the Prevention of Cruelty to Children, and to the National Hospital for Consumption at Newcastle, Co. Wicklow, is irreparable. A man of sterling honesty and steadfastness of purpose, be fought for what he believed to be right, fearless of consequences and often to his own disadvantage. To all inner circle of intimate friends he was endeared by the nobility of his character – one might often have occasion to differ from him, but never to doubt or mistrust him. His life was a continuous self-sacrifice to duty, Of him it may well be said in the words of Horace – "Multis ille bonis flebilis occident." J.W. Moore.

Cecil Thomas Grimshaw – Soldier

Cecil Thomas Wrigley Grimshaw was born in Dublin, Ireland in 1875. Like his brothers he was educated at Trinity College and then joined the army. He served in the Royal Dublin Fusiliers during the Boer War during which time he kept a very interesting diary. This diary recounts his experiences in the battle of Talana, and subsequently as a prisoner of war in Pretoria at the same time as Winston Churchill. Being the first of modern warfare it is worth recounting the event.

"As back ground the South African War, also called Boer War, or Anglo-Boer War (Oct. 11, 1899 - May 31, 1902), war fought between Great Britain and the two Boer (Afrikaner) republics - the South African Republic (Transvaal) and the Orange Free State. Although it was the largest and most costly war in which the British engaged between the Napoleonic Wars and World War I, it was fought between wholly unequal protagonists. The total British military strength in South Africa reached nearly 500,000 men, whereas the Boers could muster no more than about 88,000. But the British were fighting in a hostile country over difficult terrain, with long lines of communications, while the Boers, mainly on the defensive, were able to use modern rifle fire to good effect, at a time when attacking forces had no means of overcoming it.

The war began on Oct. 11, 1899, following a Boer ultimatum directed against the reinforcement of the British garrison in South Africa. The crisis was caused by the refusal of the South African Republic, under President Paul Kruger, to grant political rights to the Uitlander (foreigners; i.e., non-Dutch and primarily English) population of the mining areas of the Witwatersrand, and the aggressive attitudes of Alfred Milner, 1st Viscount Milner, the British high commissioner, and of Colonial Secretary Joseph Chamberlain, in response to this obduracy. An underlying cause of the war was the presence in the Transvaal of the largest gold-mining complex in the world, beyond direct British control, at a time when the world's monetary systems, preeminently the British, were increasingly dependent upon gold.

The course of the war can be divided into three periods. During the first phase, the British in South Africa were unprepared and militarily weak. Boer armies attacked on two fronts, into Natal from the Transvaal and into the northern Cape from the Orange Free State; the northern districts of the Cape Colony rebelled against the British and joined the Boer forces. In the course of Black Week (December 10-15) the Boers defeated the British in a number of major engagements and besieged the key towns of Ladysmith, Mafeking, and Kimberley; but large numbers of British reinforcements were being landed, and slowly the fortunes of war turned. Before the siege of Ladysmith could be relieved, however, the British suffered another reverse at Spion Kop (January 1900).

In the second phase, the British, under Lord Kitchener and Frederick Sleigh Roberts, 1st Earl Roberts, relieved the besieged towns, beat the Boer armies in the field, and rapidly advanced up the lines of rail transportation. Bloemfontein was occupied by the British in February 1900, and Johannesburg and Pretoria in May and June. Kruger left the Transvaal for Europe. But the war, which until then had been largely confined to military operations, was by no means at an end, and at the end of 1900 it entered upon its most destructive phase. For 15 months Boer commandos, under the brilliant leadership of generals such as Christiaan Rudolf de Wet and Jacobus Hercules De la Rey, harried the British army bases and communications; large rural areas of the Transvaal and the Orange Free State (which the British annexed as the Orange River Colony) remained out of British control.

Kitchener responded with barbed wire and blockhouses along the railways, but when these failed he retaliated with a scorched-earth policy. The farms of Boers and Africans alike were destroyed and the Boer inhabitants of the countryside were rounded up and held in segregated concentration camps. The plight of the Boer women and children in these camps became an international outrage - more than 20,000 died in the carelessly run, unhygienic camps. The commandos continued their attacks, many of them deep into the Cape Colony, General Jan Smuts leading his forces to within 50 miles (80 km) of Cape Town. But Kitchener's drastic and brutal methods slowly paid off. The Boers had unsuccessfully sued for peace in March 1901; finally, they accepted the loss of their independence by the Peace of Vereeniging in May 1902."

Cecil who was 24 at the time was in the war from the beginning and was captured early on at the battle of Talana on October 20th 1899; He was interned in a prisoner of war camp in Pretoria.

Here follows his diary of the events leading to his capture and eventual release.

"During September 1899 rumours of war with the Transvaal were getting more and more prevalent & there appeared to be more truth in them, than previously. On the evening of the 16th (September) we received orders that our Mounted Infantry company to which I belonged was to leave (at that time they were stationed in Pietermaritzburg) for Ladysmith on the following Tuesday the 19th & to march up. This did not give us much time to get ready. However things worked out alright & everything was packed and we marched off passing the Quarter Guard at about 6.30 am. We had, as well as our company transport, all the regimental transport carts and wagons. We did a very good march and ended it at Dangle Road where we halted for the night.

Next morning we started off for Nottingham Road & arrived there in very good time, but some of the transport got stuck on the road opposite George Melster's farm, owing to heavy rain which came on shortly after our arrival; making the road at that spot, where it was very heavy in ordinary times, almost impassable for heavy wagons. The result was that the wagons had to stay there all night with Lt. Parmry, regimental transport officer, in charge. However we got them all out by 9 next morning & fed and watered & started off again for Mooi River, our next camp which we reached in pouring rain, but just managed to get our tents up before the place was very wet. Next morning we were on the move again for Estcourt, a very long and tedious march, but we did it in very good time, arriving with all the transport about 3.30 pm. There we again camped & next morning left for Colenso, the hottest & driest march we had, here we camped again & spent all the next day (Sunday) resting.

I may mention that after Mooi River we took very great military precautions in case of anything unforeseen cropping up of a dangerous nature. Here at Colenso we got the first news of anything disquieting. About midnight a telegram came for Capt. Lonsdale telling him to "Endeavour to reach Ladysmith with transport". Previous to this we had heard a rumour that our regiment had been sent up in a great hurry to Dundee or Glencoe, so we were more or less on the alert, expecting to hear something. Well this telegram did not effect us very much at the time, it simply meant us leaving punctually & making no mistake about getting to Ladysmith the next day. However early next morning our Color-Sergeant brought in another telegram which had arrived at 2.00 am but was not given to him till then (about 5.30 am.). This telegram said "My previous wire should have meant that you should reach here by 11 am". As soon as we got this I went out with orders from Lonsdale to get ready to start as soon as possible. This we did & after a forced march over pretty steep hills we reached Ladysmith at the right time, which was very creditable considering we had all the transport with us.

On our arrival at Ladysmith we of course found our regiment gone & it took the authorities a long time to decide where we were to be put, and to our astonishment they wanted us to go on another march to Sunday's River at once, but Lonsdale said we couldn't, which was quite right, as the transport mules were rather done after such a hard march. We eventually occupied the lines our regiment had been in & the ponies were put in the RA (Royal Artillery) stables.

We, the officers, were very kindly & hospitably looked after by the Liverpool Regiment. Next morning we had to start again for Sunday's River. I went over to the AGC stores to draw rations etc. our Color Sergeant having failed to get anything out of them. I found when I arrived, the place in a state of chaos & the storeman half drunk, with the result that I had to get the keys from him & issue the stores myself. I might have taken the whole place away for all he knew or seemed to care, but I had the form from the office with the amounts on, so I was alright. At last we started off for Sunday's River & arrived there about 4.30 pm after a very long march.

Here we spent an awful night, with rain, wind, no tents, & had to keep a strong guard & piquets out.

Next morning we started off again for Dundee & when we got to Glencoe Pass it began to rain & it was really wonderful how the mules got the wagons up it all, but we arrived alright about 4 pm. On the way through the pass we met a Boer trekking in his wagon. With all his family & a MP came along & searched it & took his rifle from him, which he first refused to give up, but eventually had to.

I was doing advanced guard this day with my section & when I got near to Glencoe Junction, I saw on the hill behind the station a lot of men whom I couldn't make out for ages. At last I discovered it was Lt. Ferreau with his company who were there on piquet, so we passed on, to Dundee camp, which turned out to be much larger than we had thought.

There were the 18th Hussars, batteries of the RA, the Leicesters & our own regiment. We were camped beside our own.

Having got the men & horses settled I took up my own abode with Erran and Shewan in their tent.

This ended our march up from Maritzburg taking in all 9 days, arriving on the 27th having left on the 19th.

For the first couple of days we rested & cleaned up the horses & everything after the march. Then we started reconnoitering for miles round Dundee, right over to the Buffalo River & up towards Newcastle. This was the daily routine, intermingled with mounted and dismounted piquets by day and by night. Then rumour began to fly about, about the Boers massing on the border etc. On the 12th October war was declared, on the night of the 13th a rumour came that the Free Staters were advancing on Ladysmith & our regiment left that night about 1.30 by train. The next day we moved our camp to higher ground on account of the heavy rains.

The regiment returned on Saturday the 14th about 10 or 11 pm having done nothing except a long march out to meet the enemy who never turned up.

This over we went on as usual with nearly every night a piquet to be furnished somewhere & we (the Subalterns took it turn about with these piquets.

One night about the 16th or 17th the KRA were sniped at by some lawless Natal Dutch & created quite an excitement. I mention this as being perhaps the reason why certain things happened afterwards.

In the afternoon of the 19th of Oct (Thursday) orders came in to us at 3.30 to furnish a picquet of 12 men on the Landsman's Drift road in the vicinity of the cross roads leading to Landsman's Drift & Barrts Drift.

I was sent for my piquet & left camp at 4.30 pm, having given the men their dinners & had the horses fed, going round by a circuitous route to my post.

Here I arrived just at dusk and I don't know why, but somehow, I thought that something was going to happen, so I fell the men in & warned them to be very careful & alert & that if anyone advanced without answering their challenge after the third time to shoot them, unless they had very good reasons for thinking they could not be heard. After this little oration I sent out my patrols warning them that I was going to move the position of my piquet after dark. This I did, leaving a sentry (double) on the road. About 7 pm it began to pour & we were all pretty well soaked through in an hour. Just about 8 pm, my sentry on the road challenged someone who did not answer, he challenged twice, but still no answer, I rushed over to see what it was & luckily recognized Mr. Robinson, one of our intelligence officers with another man & two bantu scouts. It was very well I did as the next moment he would have been shot as the sentry had loaded & I had drawn my revolver ready to shoot.

I asked him why he had not answered & he said he had passed my scouts & told them who he was & thought that was alright.

He had never been given any "countersign" or anything, & if I had not happened to have known him from meeting him sometime before at polo it might have been a very serious thing. However from him I learned that a force of Boers, about 200 strong, had moved across Mulamgeni Mountain about 6 miles to my front, moving in a southerly direction. This seemed to be all he knew about them, but it was quite enough for me, as I knew that there was a commando behind the Doorneberg, so it kept me on the "gin-some". All went quite smoothly & at 1.30 am I relieved my patrol, or rather sent out the relief.

Just after the old relief had come in & settled down, I heard horses hoofs clattering on the road some distance out in front, as if they had galloped off the veldt across the road & on to the veldt again. I turned to my sentry & asked him if he had heard it, & he said "yes! It sounded like horses".

About 10 minutes after this I heard my patrol out in front challenging and getting no answer. They challenged three times Then they fired and I knew the show had begun as their fire was returned at once. As soon as my patrol was clear I opened fire & kept it up for a bit on the mounted figures of men in front, as soon as the enemy's bullets began coming near the piquet all the ponies who were linked went off like a streak of lightening knocking down their guard & cleared.

The Boers came on, I should think there were about 20 of

them & I retired slowly back up the hill towards the neck keeping off the road, which I maintained saved us, as we had heard the bullets pinging on the road to our left.

After the second retirement I found one of my men lying on the ground & asked him what was the matter. He said he was shot & I said where, he said in the arm. I tried to get him to rise and walk as we were being fired on heavily & had to retire, but he said "Oh Christ, I am shot let me die". This shows you what a trouble he was. So I had to lift him up & got him back behind the firing line & then opened fire again on the Boers, who seemed to be increasing in number & I thought trying to get round us to cut us off. Here I suddenly spied a lot of our horses up against the line & I left the men in position with Sergeant Guilfoyle who was a wrotter, but I would not trust any of the men to catch the horses & I went round got behind them & fortunately found my mare was still with them. I called to her & she knew me at once, & let me come up to her, & as the others were all tied to her I captured the lot of them. Four had gone altogether, then I returned the men on them & again tried to get Pte. Brenman who was wounded up on one & send him in, but he refused. First of all I forgot to say I sent my sergeant in on one of the horses as far as he could go to take a message to the effect that we had been attacked & were retiring on the neck, that the Boers appeared to be advancing in large numbers.

Well as Pte Brenman refused or would not stay on the horse when I put him up there was nothing to do but to carry him; so in this way we reached the neck. As soon as we got down behind the neck & knew we were safe from being cut off, I sent Pte. Brenman back with four men to carry him.

Having got them off I then mounted the four remaining men and advanced up to the neck again to try & find one of my patrols which had got lost & I thought might be hiding somewhere & that we might get him away, but as we got up on the neck again the Boers fired at us from the hill on the right of the road, & drove us back. It was just daylight by this time & we could see the Boers lining the hills so I sent another man in with a message to that effect. Then the Boers started sniping at us & eventually we had to withdraw to the sand Spruit at the edge of the town.

I could not make out what had happened or why it was no one came out to relieve or support us. I had all my men in except one who I kept with me at the Spruit. Eventually I decided to go back & find out if everything was being done & left the one man on the Spruit. As I had got a little way into town I met one of my men who was coming back with a message to say that there were two companies coming to my support.

These I met, commanded by Capts Welden and Dibley. Welden sent me to recall his advance guard to the Spruit, which by that time had advanced towards the hill. Then he sent me out with 3 or 4 men as scouts to guard his front and flanks while he was deploying his 2 companies.

I was then employed in carrying messages between Welden and Dibley when suddenly we saw some mounted men on our left flank & Welden sent me out to find out what they were, & we discovered they were the Cavalary Piquet coming in from Lehulty's farm & were going up to Selana Hill to see who it was on the top when they were fired on and retired. This news I took to Weldon & then asked him if I would take my men & horses &myself in to feed &clean up ready to start out again.

Just as I got into the town the Boer's pitched a shell just in the rear of the Sandspruit where Dibley had a section of his company.

As I came up through the town & got to the market square another shell pitched in the market square which made all the people scuttle away who had crowded out to see the show. Then as I got into camp there were shells flying about all over the place & having reported myself to the Adjutant, I went in search of my company. This I found had been moved in the rear of a small koppie. Having found my groom with my second charger I changed on to him and left 'Gipsy" with Kelly to be taken care of, & fed, & told him & McDarly, my servant, that they had better go out with their companies. I then went off and joined my company.

Just after I arrived with my company we got orders to move off with the 18th Hussars under Col. Moller to do a flank attack on the enemy's right rear.

We started off & were shelled heavily by the Boers from Talana Hill, crossing the open, but eventually arrived under cover on the Sandspruit. There we halted for a few minutes &were then ordered to move on again & galloped across the open again being shelled till we arrived under cover of a small koppie on the Boers' right flank. This was an ideal position for taking the enemy in the flank and rear & our company dismounted & the cavalry machine gun came up on our left. We had not been there five minutes & were just going to open fire when for some unknown reason we were taken away, by an order of Col. Moller sent by Lt. Shore AVD, he having previously taken his regiment away on account of some rumour of some Boers being down below us.

There was a thick mist & for some time we could not find the cavalry but eventually found them dismounted in the middle of the plain in the rear of the enemy's position. Here we also dismounted. After a couple of minutes a party of Boers appeared on the main road on our left rear as we looked at Talana & Lonsdale told me to take my section over & capture them.

This I did extending my section fan shaped & going round them. In rear of this party of Boers was an ambulance & rear of it again another party of Boers about 6 or 8 in number. These to my astonishment I saw being charged by one of the squadrons that was then left with us, as the other two had gone I don't know where. It seemed to me an awful shame this squadron charging with drawn swords on those few men, who were quite ready to give in, but nevertheless were slashed & cut by our sabers. These men were then brought up to where other prisoners were & were dismounted, their arms taken from them & put in our medical store cart, which heaven only knows how it followed us over the country it did, The prisoners I was ordered to tie together with rope & take the braces off. Then at last we were dismounted and told to take up a position on the south of Landsman's Drift road absolutely in the open without any cover & for the first time opened fire on the enemy's rear, it long range, drawing all their fire on to us, as at that time they were retiring from Talana Hill. The result was that we had very soon to leave & were driven back to another position, this also was an absolutely rotten one & consequently had to leave it in a few minutes. From there we retired to another, & this we had to leave by the Boers coming around our right flank, & we retired then on to another position, which was our last in that phase of the fight. This was a very good one & we held the Boers in check & they were actually going back, but still Moller, who was in the rear of where I was with the lead horses & could not see anything, ordered us to retire, which took sometime to be carried out as no one seemed to understand.

He first called out to retire & I who had kept galloping forward from the lead horses to see how things were getting on & saw it was alright took no notice, till he came closer & called to me individually to tell them to retire. So I galloped up to the firing line & even Lonsdale could not understand what was meant, & took sometime to order the retirement, wanting to know the reason for it. I said I did not know, but Col Moller had ordered it. This position was the only one in which the cavalry ever fired a shot & they had a splendid opportunity of manouvering round our right flank & rolling up the enemy, but no advantage was taken of it. However from this position we retired through a narrow neck over the sand river leaving the machine gun behind without anyone to look after it. A section of the RRR's had been taken off the machine gun, but earlier in the day it was taken away & put on the exactly opposite flank & consequently when the company was withdrawn the machine gun was left alone, eventually falling into the hands of the Boers, all the machine gun section being either killed or wounded.

Having passed through this neck we were perfectly safe from the Boers, & as we were driven off our best plan naturally was to return to camp, but in spite of all advice & remonstrations about going back either in front of or behind Inyati Mountain, we were galloped on I believe with a view to striking the Newcastle Road & eventually ran into Grasine's commando who then attacked us & we were obliged to take up position, or rather Col Moller insisted on taking up a position, on a spur of Inyati Mountain. Then the Boers began to close round us & after a lot of difficulty I got our horses under cover by distributing them about behind little elevations & rocks.

This being done I took nearly all the No 3s away leaving the horses in charge of Sergeant Fletcher & as few men as possible, sufficient to hold them,& sent the others under Sergeant Caroll, to drive the Boers back from Le Mesurier's left. This we succeeded to do, but it merely had the effect of driving them back further onto the plain & they then went up another spur of Inyati Mountain & were coming around in our rear. Seeing this I at once went down &told Col. Moller & suggested that if we wanted to get away we ought to go then, & showed him the direction; but he said no, that some of his horses were shot so he could not go. At this time there were only three shot, & we could easily have managed to have taken three men on our own horses. We might, & probably would have lost some men, but it would have been better than loosing the whole lot. Then I wanted him to let me go and get help, but no, I was not let. Then the Boers shelling us, & eventually we had to surrender, which came as a surprise to us, & did not seem to surprise or worry our Commanding Officer, who seemed to take it all in the days work. I know I and the others never felt so bad in our lives, as we and all the men were prepared to fight to the end, instead of being handed over as we were to the Boers, as a present.

After a lot of counting & worrying & being stripped of our swords, revolvers & everything, & one man even wanted me to hand over my rings, but I stuck at that. After all was over we found that we had two men killed, one in the 18th Hussars killed & nine wounded altogether, & 15 18th Hussars horses more or less wounded & had to be shot.

Then we were marched off to the Boers' Laage at the navigation Collieries where we were put in the dining room of a sort of store hotel, with a guard, & really were very kindly treated, though of course pretty rough. Here we spent the night, sleeping on mattresses on the floor, In the morning we were brought a lot of hot coffee, milled bread, biscuits, etc. Then about 10.30 we were driven to Dannhauser station, on buchs wagons & put in the train, & started off to Pretoria where we arrived the following morning the 22nd October (my birthday) about 12 o'clock.

There we were met by an enthusiastic crowd, evidently awfully pleased at such a haul of prisoners, altogether men & officers 174. Then we were marched off to the racecourse by a circuitous route, with crowds of people to look at us. On arriving at the racecourse we were put in a tin shed place, used as a lunch room at race meetings & the men were put in the grandstand. At first we were not allowed to go outside the enclosure, but eventually we were allowed to walk about in the garden attached. Of course we had a guard round us & at night were not allowed outside the enclosure.

Then we started our prison life & I was made mess president & looked after the cooking & feeding for the officers. I also did quartermaster for the men & issued their rations every day. We did practically the same every day, walking up and down the garden, reading, feeding, & sleeping. Then on Wednesday the 1st of November, the officers and men of the 12th battalion of 1st Gloucestershire Regiment & 1st Battalion of Grenadier Fusiliers arrived. Altogether about 40 officers & 900 men. Then the work and worry began. The officers I had to feed in reliefs as I only had kit in the way of plates etc for 10, but we got through it alright. It was quite evident there was no room for all these people there, so next day they moved us from there to Staats Model School. I was sent on in front to tell off the rooms etc. and get things ready for the others when they arrived.

Then we settled down to the routine of this place which consisted in walking round & round the house & reading & sleeping & feeding. By degrees our numbers were increased by no fence. We were first told on the 31st that the British would be in tomorrow & we would be released. This proved to be a fallacy as they did not come for a week & that week we spent all day watching the hills round for our tr_ & that on the 4th June we saw our own shells bursting on the hills all round & one Lyddite gun dropped shells right in the hills. Then at about 4 am out to Churchill & the Duke of Marlborough galloped up. We saw them coming & rushed out en masse, seized the guard & put them inside & I climbed up the flagstaff with a Union Jack in my teeth & tied it on at the head. This one was made by Brownlow in prison & was the first one over Pretoria. Then we went down the town. Next day the men arrived & we were made into Provisional battalions. We were after that sent down to June to guard the bridge that had been blown up & stayed there about a week, then we went down to Kroonstad, i.e. our own men & remounted & went round the Free State after de Wet. Then we came up to Pretoria & went north then back again down West, then

Cecil's account of the Duke of Marlborough and Winston Churchill at the capture of Pretoria (Boer War).

***Cecil climbing the flagpole with the Union Jack in his mouth -
June 1st 1900. Illustrated London News.***

batches of officers arriving, numbering from 1 to 13, till now the total number is 103. Here we were guarded by 2 ARP's who treated us as criminals & when we complained of it nothing was done. The officers complained a good deal of their treatment altogether, but they did not seem to realize that the Boers, who called themselves civilized, certainly were not as regard to their treatment of people in our position & did not understand us. They thought if we got the same as their men did on the veldt it was all that could be expected. They did not go on the ordinary civilized formula of doing all they could to alleviate our unhappy misfortune, due generally to the fault of some senior officers & not to the individuals.

Then the next thing that occurred of note was Churchill's escape. This he did, as all the world knows, but they do not know that he did it contrary to the agreement of his mates, who were to escape with him; & so instead of 20 officers getting away, as they might easily have done, as there was no one to know whether they were there or not, except myself; he was the only one from the School. After his escape all sorts of restrictions were put on, newspapers stopped etc. Then we started a system of signaling, with the people across the road. We got the latest and best wires to the Transvaal from their officials who told it to the people across the road, and they signaled it to us. Then all went on as usual. Prisoners kept arriving & we got the latest news, generally twice a day. Then Haldane, Les Mesieurir & I arranged to cut the wire to escape, but there was still one light which we could not get out. This proved to be worse than we hoped & when the lights did go out & we were half way across the yard, we found ourselves in bright light & had to double back again. Then there was nothing for it but wait till we were to go. But Haldane & Le M who slept in a different room from me had a hole in the floor & down this they went that same night, with the result that the next morning when they were missed, they all thought that they had escaped under cover of darkness by the wires being cut. Well there they stayed for 3 weeks & I fed them every day. Then on March 15th we were moved to the tin shed on the north of the town. Here we did much the same as before, but we had more outdoor room & played cricket of sorts & one day had sports.

Then the last week of our captivity was one of suspense. We were first told on the 31st that the British would be in tomorrow & we would be released. This proved to be a fallacy as they did not come for a week & that week we spent all day watching the hills round for our troops, and then on the 4th June we saw shells bursting on the hills all round, & one lydati gun dropped shells right over the hills. Then about 4 am on the 5th Churchill & the Duke of Marlborough galloped up. We saw them coming & rushed out en masse seized the guard & put them inside & I climbed up the flagstaff with a Union Jack in my teeth & tied it on at the head. This was made by Burrowes in prison & was the first one over Pretoria.

Then we went down the town. Next day the men arrived & we were made into provisional battalions. We were after that sent down to Irene to guard the bridge that had been blown up, & stayed there about 8 weeks. Then we went down to Kroonstad, & found our own men & remounted, & went round the Free State after de Wet. Then we came up to Pretoria & went north, then back again & out west with Ian Hamilton to Commando Neck on his way to Rustenburg, & the rest of the state & of Hickman's force, to which we belonged went to Irene. There I joined them about the middle of August & have been here ever since".

In his semi-autobiographical work <u>London to Ladysmith via Pretoria</u>, Winston Churchill states: "A very energetic and clever young officer of the Dublin Fusiliers, Lieutenant Grimshaw, undertook the task of managing the mess, and when he was assisted by another subaltern - Lieutenant Southey, of the Royal Irish Fusiliers, this became an exceedingly well-conducted concern. In spite of the high prices prevailing in Pretoria - prices which were certainly not lowered for our benefit - the somewhat meagre rations which the government allowed were supplemented, until we lived, for three shillings a day, quite as well as any regiment on service."

Cecil was awarded the Distinguished Service Order (D.S.O)

Cecil Thomas Wrigley Grimshaw D.S.O was born in Dublin, Ireland in 1875. He was killed in action at Gallipoli on April 26th 1915.

for his gallantry and service in this war. He was promoted to Captain on July 14th 1904 and on December 28th 1911 was appointed Adjutant of 1st Battalion, Royal Dublin Fusiliers, a position he still held when the Great War erupted, the Battalion then being garrisoned at Madras, India.

After the Boer War, he passed through Alexandria, Egypt, where he met and fell in love with Agnes Violet Alderson who he later married on October 3rd 1906.

Agnes Violet Alderson on her wedding day - October 3rd 1906 to Cecil Thomas Wrigley Grimshaw D.S.O.

Violet – The Girl from Alexandria

Agnes Violet Alderson, known to her family as Violet, was born in Alexandria, Egypt, in 1885. She was the youngest but one of a family of ten children, with five brothers and four sisters. Her father George Beeton Alderson had gone to Egypt in 1863 at the age of 19. He was employed by Ransomes, Sims and Jeffries of Ipswich. Their entry for him in their Register was: "Wages increased to 8/- 19.9.1863" and the next entry read "gone to Egypt". It seems he was taking out a consignment of Agricultural Machinery to Samuel Stafford Allen, who by then was running his own business in Egypt, having himself previously been trained by Ransomes. George Alderson quickly realized the opportunities for business that existed there. The business was the supply of pumping machinery to farmers to replace the age old water wheels and hoists which the fellaheen had used since time immemorial to lift water from the Nile to irrigate their land. He was an engineer and was able to convince the then Chairman of Ruston and Hornsby to make him their agent. He called at Ruston's house when he was in bed on a Sunday night and asked for an agency for Egypt for 10,000 to 20,000 pounds. Ruston told him from the bedroom window to go away. GBA said, *"but I have got the cash!"* Ruston replied *"wait a minute young man, I'm coming down"* - and so he did, presumably in night cap and gown! The cash seems to have come from great friends of his grandmother Ann Alderson (nee Beeton). He got the agency anyway and

Allen Alderson & Co machinery store at Alexandria harbour. Circa 1900. Note the square riggers in the background.

Norland House, Aboukir, Alexander, Egypt, circa 1900. The home of George Alderson.

was sufficiently successful to be able to establish a nice home in which to rear his family. "Articles of Partnership" were drawn up between S. Stafford Allen and G.B. Alderson in 1869. Later Allen Alderson and Co. was formed by Francis Allen (Stafford's son) and G.B. Alderson. The firm finally closed down shortly after World War II.

Violet used to say that she was very spoilt as a girl - perhaps because of her being the youngest daughter, perhaps because she and her next older sister were quite strikingly good looking. She was able, for instance, to collect a nice library of leather bound classics, (now in the possession of her granddaughter Patsy). The books are housed in a glass-fronted bookcase, possibly a wedding present from her Violet. There is a neat alphabetical list in a notebook dated January 10th, 1907. The collection included several prizes from her time at Upper St. Leonard's Ladies College 1901 - 1902; Macaulay's Essays for English Class 1, Milton, Senior Tennis Prize and Wordsworth - as a reward of Merit Easter 1902. She also rode and played tennis as much as she liked. She used to enjoy riding out to the Pyramids, though this must have been when staying with some of the family in Cairo. Her elder sister Eva was married to Tim Richmond and they had their home there. It was an indication of George Alderson's entrepreneurial flair that he purchased the hulk of a French battleship, that had been sunk at the Battle of the Nile, had it refloated and anchored in Aboukir Bay as a houseboat. It was called "The

Mabel Harsden and Violet Alderson, later Mrs Herbert Alderson and Mrs. Cecil Grimshaw

Ark" and was evidently the scene of many happy swimming parties. Violet learnt to swim from it by being put in the water supported by two gourds.

Their home was Norland House, named after Norland Place, Notting Hill, the home of Ellen Wells whom George Alderson had married in 1869. They evidently had a number of staff as was usual in 'colonial' households of those days. There certainly was a butler. Many years later when Violet returned to Egypt in the 1920's after an absence of 18 years this retainer was distressed that she had forgotten the Arabic she used to be able to speak. However, one day when she was making a telephone call and the operator was being more dilatory than usual, she let fly quite a torrent of Arabic down the mouthpiece! Just at this moment the old butler appeared in the doorway and said, "I thought Memsahib had forgotten all her Arabic"!

Her schooling probably followed the usual pattern for those days and was carried out by tutors and governesses. Though she must have spent time at school in England. Peter Alderson (a nephew) has a letter from his mother about her meeting with Violet at "School in St. Leonards (Sussex) in 1898". "Met Violet there and stayed with them at Kew in Christmas and Easter holidays and she came to us in summer.

Her bookcase contained prizes for 1901-1902. She certainly could speak French quite well, and some Italian. Her handwriting was bold and flowing and she had a good command of her own language. She was also able to play the piano and her son David recalls how he used to love her playing De Souza marches when he was quite small. The arts must have played quite a part in her upbringing as her parents would take the family to Paris, Bayreuth and Salzburg for holidays.

George Alderson was awarded a K.B.E. in 1922 for services in connection with Egypt. His first wife Ellen (nee Wells) died just before Violet's wedding in 1906. In his latter years he married a Greek lady from the Ponsetta family of Corfu. She recalled that George Alderson had always enjoyed cordial relations with the Egyptian people with whom he did business, and that he concluded many deals with a simple handshake. His customers never let him down.

Sir George Alderson died in 1926. At a service in All Saints Church, Bulkeley to dedicate a memorial tablet, Bishop Gwynne of Egypt and the Sudan described him as one of a band of early British pioneers who went to Egypt in the mid 19th Century, "*He was*", the Bishop said, "*a man of great means, and an open-handed, very generous man. He made a good deal of money, but he spent it freely on all sorts of people. He was a great benefactor to Victoria College; the friends he made he always stuck to. He had been instrumental in the building of this church*". He had also made donations to the Sailors' Home, to the Blind School, to the Mosque at Aboukir for a Minaret and to the Public Baths.

Cecil and Violet Grimshaw – Army Life

Cecil and Violet remained in Ireland from December 1906 to November 1908. Their guest book records quite a lot of comings and goings, and of course they were not far from Thomas Wrigley Grimshaw, Cecil's father, at that time established in Carrickmines near Dublin.

Cecil's regiment in those days, the Dublin Fusiliers, was part of the British Army, the English Army. At the beginning of the 20th Century Ireland was not an independent country.

The first years of married life in Ireland were difficult ones for Violet. She enjoyed the hunting and riding, but found the cold and damp unpleasant after her upbringing in Egypt. Her first child, Tommy, was conceived early on in Ireland and this put an end for the time being to her riding and social life, much to her disgruntlement. Tommy, was born at Buttevant, Cork the Regimental Base. The adjustment to living on the income of an Army Captain was also a difficult one, as she had been used to having almost anything she wanted whilst under her father's roof.

Violet was an accomplished horsewoman, here at Buttevant (1907), Co Cork, Ireland

They remained in Ireland from December 1906 to November 1909.

The 1st Battalion of the Dublins was sent out to India in January 1910. They were posted first to Poona (now Pune) and Ahmednagar. Violet and Tommy accompanied Cecil and the next few years were happy and active ones. They had their own Bungalow at Ahmednagar, near Poona and a numerous household of Indian servants. There was plenty of excitement and Violet reveled in the horse riding - she was adept at tilting at the ring while Cecil carried off the prizes for tent pegging. There were bridge parties and dinner parties and the wives got together over afternoon teas. The British Raj was still at the height of its power. Their second son, George, was born on September 8th 1910, at Ahmednagar.

Cecil was present at the Delhi Durbar when King George V was enthroned as Emperor of India in 1911. His Durbar Medal is amongst the family possessions. These halcyon days were not to last for long. In March 1912 Violet, Tommy and George sailed for England. The letter Cecil wrote after their departure showed what a very devoted couple they were. Cecil was quite heart broken at the parting. He wrote on his return to his hotel:

Taj Mahal Palau Hotel Bombay, March 1st, 1912

"My Own Darling,
Just a line to say I am off to Nagar to my terrible loneliness. No Girlie, No Tommy, No George, all a wilderness. But we spent two happy days together here anyway Darling. There was someone in Tommy's room already when I got back from the boat, and the hotel crowded when I went down to dinner, all people from the P & O. Goodbye Darling little love. I hope the next time I am here will be to meet you, unless I win the Derby sweep and then it will be to go to you. If your Dad really wants to do a charitable act get him to settle £500 pounds a year on us and I will come home at once. I can't stand this. Your loving boy, Cecil"

1st Battalion, Dublin Fusiliers, at Nuneaton, February 1915, just prior to embarkation for Gallipoli. Major Cecil Grimshaw D.S.O. sitting 6th from right.

The letter was addressed c/o Geo B Alderson Esq, where Violet was staying with her father in Egypt on the her way back to England.

Back in England Violet, handed George and Tommy over to Granny (Sarah) Grimshaw, Cecil's mother, at The Lodge, Waterbeach, not far from Cambridge. Sarah had been a widow since 1906 and had all her own family and endless cousins turning up at Waterbeach (5 miles north of Cambridge on the Ely Road). George, who was one at the time, had no recollections of staying, but was told that once he was sick in a horse drawn carriage on a shopping trip to Cambridge which didn't make him very popular. In 1912 nobody had cars except for very exceptional people, in fact it was rather superior to have a coachman and a brougham and to go shopping in it.

Sarah Grimshaw and grandsons at Waterbeach, circa 1912

Violet returned to India by herself and joined Cecil in Ahmednagar in October 1912. In February 1913 the Regiment returned to Fort St George in Madras (now Chennai) where the regiment had its origins as the Madras Regiment of the East India Company, and later became known as Neil's Blue Caps. The latter had left Madras in 1857 to join the forces helping to relieve Cawnpore at the time of the Indian Mutiny. They had not returned since. So there were great celebrations in Madras when they arrived.

In May 1913 Violet returned to England because they knew a European war was imminent and she took the "Old Cottage" (made of flint stone) on the village square in Upper Sheringham (Norfolk - 25 miles north of Norwich and a mile

George, Violet and Tommy. Upper Sheringham, September 1913

from the sea), the latter had a water trough in the middle, because horses were the only means of transport, and there was a church on the other side of the village square. The round horse trough, church and cottage are still there. The church is located in the centre of the village and dates back to the 15th century, although there has been a church on the site for over a thousand years. There were guns up in the nearby park and the soldiers used to bring their horses down every day to be watered. George used to go out and see them. George remembered the soldiers wearing riding breeches and puttees. On one occasion when out walking with the governess, a very sinister looking man started walking ahead of them towards the park, they followed him, and said he was a spy! They had a very happy time in Upper Sheringham.

The only outstanding incident George recalls being told about was his getting lost in Sheringham while Violet was shopping, and she hectically started searching Sheringham for him. Panic as usual. Years later on board a ship going to Africa George's son Christopher was lost. Nobody could find Christopher until eventually he was found down with the cook. In George's case he was found in the baker's shop, sitting there stuffing himself with cream buns.

Various cousins used to come and stay with them and there are photos of Violet going off on a motor car trip with Uncle Bertie, who was Chief Justice in Cyprus at that time. He died later because he pumice stoned a corn on his foot and got septicemia. Pumice stones were all the rage then. That was the only way one could remove a corn!.

At that time Cecil was still in India. After Violet left him there she received a letter from him (knowing the War was coming some time soon and he didn't know whether he would see her or not, telling her that there was £100 in Cox & King Bank and that ought to see her through the war!. Cecil in Madras was very much hoping Violet would be able to come to him again in India. He was very torn. The following year as he had applied for a posting that would give him a better chance of active service and promotion. He half hoped the job would not come off, as if it did he would not be able to have his wife join him. Although he was offered the job and was making all arrangements in readiness to join his new unit, other orders must have come posting his Battalion back to England.

Cecil Wrigley Grimshaw with Tommy (b 1907) and George (b. 1910) at Nuneaton in February 1915

The Dublin Fusiliers were brought home in 1914. There were a lot of troop movements in those days. They may have swapped battalions and just brought some of the officers home or something, The family was at Nuneaton (near Birmingham) in January 1915 where the Irish Brigade were training to go off to war. There are photos of Cecil with Tommy and George in uniform - in those days regimental tailors made children's uniforms.

George never remembered his Father in the flesh at all, and only remembers him from photographs.

Violet and Cecil Grimshaw at Numeaton Jan 24th 1915. Last photo of them together.

The regiment went off to war from Nuneaton, but on the way they laid up their colours, in the Roman Catholic church in Torquay; because, of course, being an Irish regiment they were mostly Catholics. There are two postcards of the Grand Harbour at Malta dated Valletta, March 2, 1915, and simply inscribed "with love from Cecil" and signed C. Grimshaw, Maj. They were addressed to Mrs. Cecil Grimshaw at The Lodge, Waterbeach, Cambridgeshire, They may have been the last messages Violet had from Cecil. He was killed in the action at Cape Hellas the day after landing at "V" Beach, the southern tip of the Gallipoli Peninsula, on April 26th 1915.

Gallipoli and the Dardanelles Campaign.

Gallipoli. (Turkish - *Gelibolu*) , historically Callipolis seaport and town, European Turkey. It lies on a narrow peninsula where the Dardanelles opens into the Sea of Marmara, 126 miles (203 km) west-southwest of Istanbul. An important Byzantine fortress, it was the first Ottoman conquest (c. 1356) in Europe and was maintained as a naval base because of its strategic importance for the defense of Istanbul. It was also a key transit station on the trade routes from Rumelia (Ottoman possessions in the Balkans) to Anatolia. In World War I, Gallipoli was the scene of determined Turkish resistance to the Allied forces during the Dardanelles Campaign, in which most of the town was destroyed. A storehouse of the Byzantine emperor Justinian (6th century), a 14th Century square castle attributed to the Ottoman sultan Bayezid I, and mounds known as the tombs of Thracian kings still stand. The new town, developed as a fishing and sardine-canning centre, is connected by road and steamer service with Istanbul and is also linked by road with Edirne. Pop. (1990 prelim.) 18,052. *"Gallipoli" Encyclopædia Britannica from Encyclopædia Britannica.*

Dardanelles Campaign. Also called Gallipoli Campaign (February 1915 - January 1916), in World War I, an Anglo-French operation against Turkey, intended to force the 38 mile (61 km) long Dardanelles channel and to occupy Constantinople. Plans for such a venture were considered by the British authorities between 1904 and 1911, but military and naval opinion was against it. When war between the Allies and Turkey began early in November 1914, the matter was reexamined and classed as a hazardous, but possible, operation.

On January 2, 1915, in response to an appeal by Grand Duke Nicholas, commanding the Russian armies, the British government agreed to stage a demonstration against Turkey to relieve pressure on the Russians on the Caucasus front. The Dardanelles was selected as the place, a combined naval and military operation being strongly supported by the then first lord of the Admiralty, Winston Churchill . On January 28 the Dardanelles committee decided on an attempt to force the straits by naval action alone, using mostly obsolete warships too old for fleet action. On February 16 this decision was modified, as it was agreed that the shores of the Dardanelles would have to be held if the fleet passed through. For this purpose a large military force under General Sir Ian Hamilton was assembled in Egypt, the French authorities also providing a small contingent. The naval bombardment began on February 16 but was halted by bad weather and not resumed until February 25. Demolition parties of marines landed almost unopposed, but bad weather again intervened. On March 18 the bombardment was continued; however, after three battleships had been sunk and three others damaged, the navy abandoned its attack, concluding that the fleet could not succeed without military help.

Troop transports assembled off the island of Lemnos, and landings began on the Gallipoli Peninsula at two places early on April 25,

1915, at Cape Helles (29th British and Royal Naval divisions) and at ANZAC beaches (Australian and New Zealand troops). A French brigade landed on the Anatolian coast opposite, at Kum Kale, but was later withdrawn. Small beachheads were secured with difficulty, the troops at ANZAC being held up by Turkish reinforcements under the redoubtable Mustafa Kemal, later to became famous as Atatürk. Large British and Dominion reinforcements followed, yet little progress was made. On August 6 another landing on the west coast, at Suvla Bay, took place; after good initial progress the assault was halted.

In May 1915 the first sea lord, Admiral Lord Fisher, had resigned because of differences of opinion over the operation. By September 1915 it was clear that without further large reinforcements there was no hope of decisive results, and the authorities at home decided to recall Hamilton to replace him by Lieutenant General Sir Charles Monroe. The latter recommended the withdrawal of the military forces and abandonment of the enterprise, advice that was confirmed in November by the secretary of state for war, Lord Kitchener, when he visited the peninsula. This difficult operation was carried out by stages and was successfully completed early on January 9, 1916.

Altogether, the equivalent of some 16 British, Australian, New Zealand, Indian, and French divisions took part in the campaign. British Commonwealth casualties, apart from heavy losses among old naval ships, were 213,980. The campaign was a success only insofar as it attracted large Turkish forces away from the Russians. The plan failed to produce decisive results because of poor military leadership in some cases, faulty tactics including complete lack of surprise, the inexperience of the troops, inadequate equipment, and an acute shortage of shells.

The campaign had serious political repercussions. It gave the impression throughout the world that the Allies were militarily inept. Before the evacuation had been decided, H.H. Asquith's Liberal administration was superseded by his coalition government. Churchill, the chief protagonist of the venture, resigned from the government and went to command an infantry battalion in France. In the end the campaign hastened Asquith's resignation, and his replacement as prime minister by David Lloyd George, in December 1916. *"Dardanelles Campaign" Encyclopædia Britannica from Encyclopædia Britannica*

Cecil Grimshaw landed at "V" Beach, a sandy strip some 9 metres wide and 320 metres long, backed along almost the whole of it's length by a low sandy escarpment about 3 metres high, where the ground almost falls nearly sheer down to the beach. Behind it is a concave grassy slope rising (at first gradually) to the cliff edge between Sedd el Bahr village and Cape Helles.

The landing at "V" Beach, in the early morning of the 25th April, 1915, was to be made by boats containing three companies of the first Royal Dublin Fusiliers, followed by the collier "River Clyde" with the rest of the Dublins, the first Royal Munster Fusiliers, half the second Hampshire Regiment, and other troops. The place was very strongly fortified, and during the

Col. R. A Rooth, Major C.T.W. Grimshaw, D.S.O., Captain B.V J. Anderson, Capt. G.M. Dunlop, Lieut. R. de Lusignan, Capt. M.J. Higginson, Lieut. B. Bernard, Lieut. W. Andrews, Rev Father W. Finn RC Chaplain 1st Bat Royal Dublin Fusiliers, k.i.a. 25th & 26th April, 1915.

25th the landing was partially carried out at the cost of very heavy casualties. On the morning of the 26th, Colonel Doughty-Wylie and Captain Walford, who were killed during the fight, had led the survivors on the beach to the capture of Sedd el Bahr village and the Old Castle above it.

On the evening of the 26th, the main body of the French Corps began to land at "V" Beach, and after the advance on the 27th the front line was nearly three kilometres beyond it. It was used as the French base during the summer.

Major Cecil Wrigley Grimshaw D.S.O. was killed on April 26th and was buried in "V" Beach Cemetery, Helles.

The cemetery stands at the bottom of the grass slope, almost touching the sand. The cemetery was begun and ended, so far as the burials are concerned in 1915, during April and May; but after the Armistice 13 graves were concentrated into Row O. It covers an area of 2,045 square metres, and it contains the graves of 500 sailors and soldiers from the United King-

"V" Beach Cemetery (2008). The Fort on the Hill in the background was the initial objective. It was in the middle ground that Cecil fell mortally wounded.

dom. The unnamed graves are 480 in number, but special memorials are erected to 196 officers and men (nearly all belonging to the units which landed on the 25th April), known or believed to be buried among them.

The Register records particulars of 216 British burials. Cecil is buried in V Beach Cemetery, Grave F11.

The family was in Guildford (Surrey) at the time and had rented rooms near the London road station. They had a governess called Miss Chissell. Violet had to go into Guildford to find out that her husband had been killed in the Gallipoli landings. Miss Chissell evidently accompanied her on this sad occasion. Violet would have been thirty, Tommy seven and George four. David had yet to be born. Miss Chissell must have been a wonderful stand by and no doubt there were other officer's wives nearby who would have been very supportive. Helen Carrington-Smith, who later married Major Donovan, was probably one of them. Violet certainly kept up with her for a long while after the war was over. The regiment was decimated at the landing and lost many officers and men so there was no room for self-pity only a courageous band of fellow sufferers.

George remembers going up stairs and finding Violet in floods of tears, poor dear, but he didn't understand what was going on. Younger brother David hadn't been born. Violet must have been carrying him at the time as he was born in October 1915.

As in the Boer War, Cecil had acquitted himself with conspicuous gallantry, leading his men up the beach in the face of withering machine-gun and rifle fire from the Turkish positions. It was said he deserved a V.C. but none of his senior officers survived to recommend him. Truth to tell, there were probably few who didn't. He was buried where he fell and some months later one of his surviving fellow officers sent home a photograph of the simple cross that had been erected.

In a letter addressed to Dear Mrs. Smiler (his wife) Stephen

J. Donovan at HQ 52nd Division wrote 19.01.16

"I met Captain Rice at Helles. He had found poor Grimmy's (Cecil) grave and took me down to it. It is quite near the RIVER CLYDE (the transport from which the Dublins had landed). Unfortunately we got pinned behind some French forage stacks as the place was heavily shelled, we decided to visit it again at a more healthy time. He had previously read the board. It had Major Grimshaw D.S.O. Dublin Fusiliers - killed in action 25t^h April 1915. - I hope to get some leave home shortly and may get an opportunity of describing this to Mrs. Grimmy".

Enclosed with the letter were three photographs perhaps taken at another time showing a Cross inscribed with the names of Col. R. A Rooth, Major C.T.W. Grimshaw, D.S.O., Captain B.V J. Anderson, Capt. G.M. Dunlop, Lieut. R. de Lusignan, Capt. M.J. Higginson, Lieut. B. Bernard, Lieut. W. Andrews, Rev Father W. Finn RC Chaplain 1st Bat Royal Dublin Fusiliers, k.i.a. 25th & 26th April, 1915. Another nearby cross commemorates 220 Officers, NCO's and men of the 1st Batt. Royal Munster Fusiliers and 1st Batt. Royal Dublin Fusiliers k.i.a. 25th & 26th April 1915. R.I.P.

The "CORK EXAMINER" of May 25th, 1915 published a report from their Cairo correspondent dated May 7th and based on accounts by men wounded in the action at Sedd El Bahr.

"Then the command was given to take the fort. The heavy guns of the fort had of course, been silenced by the fleet, but it was holding about 200 of the enemy with machine guns. Major Grimshaw, of the Dublins, was now making himself very conspicuous, moving about courageously in the open, and rallying his men together. The Dublins, with the Munsters on their left, and the Hants on their right assaulted the fort. Lieutenant Bastard, of the Dublins, now did a very brave thing - he ran fearlessly to the opening in the fort and repeatedly fired his revolver, the fire from the fort became reduced. He escaped miraculously. Soon after, the British rushed the fort and cleared out the enemy.

After this came the attack on the hill, from where the troops had been subjected to such heavy firing - One of the soldiers who participated in the attack said that Major Grimshaw continually rallied his men, exposing himself throughout. He also said that there was a Colonel with a cane in his hand going amongst the troops encouraging them, and it was he who led the men in their bayonet fight up the hill. The British completely routed the Turks and established themselves on the hill, but the brave colonel and the gallant Major Grimshaw who had done so much to ensure the success of the attack, were found dead on the field of battle".

Violet Grimshaw – A Young widow with a young family

Violet never married again. She was courted by some chap who used to turn up and they would sit together on the porch. Any rate he used to come for a bit, then he disappeared. She became friends with a woman musician, Mrs. Poe, they used to play duets on a grand piano and they sort of got chummy, Nobody was quite sure of their relationship.

It was a terrible blow for his Violet with "two & half children and only married a few years". She was only a young girl really. She had spent most of her life in Egypt where she'd had a very luxurious life. She had recovered a bit and she lived near Uncle O'Donnell who had two daughters who were much the same age as my Violet; she eventually rented a house in Dewhurst, at the cross roads between Dewhurst and Cranley, and she and her young family were there for a bit, between the time Cecil was killed in April and the Summer when they moved to Grattons. When she was at Dewhurst she made friends, (she was very good at making friends), with some people who lived in a house between Dewhurst, Cranley and Dunsfold.

Grandfather Alderson, as soon as he heard of her loss, sent her enough money to buy a home. She found a house with six acres of ground in the little Surrey village of Dunsfold. It was called "Hawera" and had belonged to a German dentist who had been interned· hence its availability.

Her Father's concern and support is shown in the letter he wrote at that time and which has fortunately been preserved. Writing on May 28th, 1915

"I hasten to relieve your anxiety and tell you I will advance the money to buy your place. As soon as you let me know I will write the Bank that amount so you can make the best terms for cash and long may you live to enjoy it with your dear ones. I shall hope one day later on to pay you a visit in your happy home, it must be from your account a charming place."

The purchase was arranged by Uncle O'Donnell and other friends of Violet, and perhaps some of her family from Egypt who were present in England, (one of her brothers was in Sussex). At any rate she hadn't a penny, she had Cecil's £100 that's all. It was quite a lot of money in those days but it wasn't going to last for ever, especially as Cox & King's Bank went bust and this money and that of various officers had deposited there for their own wives was lost. Fortunately Grandfather Alderson, who was a very rich man and gave her an allowance.

Violet moved to Dunsfold in the summer of 1915. She renamed the house "Grattons", taking the name from a pond on the village green at one corner of the property. David, the youngest of the three boys was born there in October of that year.

Gratton is the Saxon name for a plot of land. It was a lovely place, and of course it was ideal for the family because in those days one could go anywhere one liked.

The next years were not easy ones. Violet had everything to learn about running her own home with very little paid help, and no knowledge of cooking. I have heard her tell how she wept tears of frustration when she could not persuade the old 'Eagle' cooking stove in the kitchen to light.

However, she soon learnt. It is a measure of her spirit that before long she had a pony and trap that she would drive into Cranleigh for shopping, two cows - a Guernsey called

"Goblin" and a Jersey called "Daisy", a goat· Gussie, a pig - Gulliver, several hives of bees, an orchard, a soft fruit cage, and a vegetable garden. How she looked after it all, goodness only knows, but one way or another she made sure they did not starve! Violet was once stung in the throat by a bee which caused much distress. There was lots of local help for haymaking. Miss Calcut replaced Miss Chissell, and Miss Mason helped outside.

The family had a wire haired terrier called "Toby" who used to keep an eye on David in his pram - one of the big old fashioned kind. David remembers standing at the end of the drive once and seeing an airship, about the only sign of war.

The house was nicely furnished and contained a number of items that were a reminder of Violet's earlier associations with Egypt and India. There were two standard lamps in the drawing room of pierced brass work. They supported two paraffin lamps at first but were later converted to electricity. There were also pictures of Egypt and china plaques and dishes which Violet had picked up in the bazaars. Then there were various hunting knives and murderous looking daggers that Cecil had collected.

Grattons, Dunsfold, circa 1920. Violet was a great gardener and garden designer

Grattons, Dunsfold, 2006. The basic design of the garden remains as planned by Violet.

How all these things were carted around is something of a mystery. Cecil was a great organiser and had a set of wooden packing cases made in which many of these items must have traveled. Another was a fine metal bound teak chest. This was the plate chest and it was fitted with trays full of compartments and all lined with green baize - the sort of thing an Indian carpenter would make in those days for a very modest sum. Cecil had a passion for silver, and had numerous cigarette boxes and photo frames which had evidently marked special occasions. Those were the days when wedding presents had to be silver, and officers on their marriage were often given a silver salver by their brother officers, so all in all he amassed quite a collection. There were sporting trophies and various household items of course.

George, David and Tommy at Gratton's circa 1917

Cecil's memory was kept very much alive, with photos, plaques and scrolls as well as his medals in places of honour around the house. Some of his uniforms, including his bearskin (busby) as well as his sporting guns and polo sticks remained in the attic for some years before being disposed of.

Violet had some good friends in the village at that time. The Rev. and Mrs. Simpson were among them. They had lost their eldest son in the war. Their daughter Joan was very friendly with Violet, and no doubt quite a support. She went out to India as a missionary and Violet kept up a correspondence with her for many years. Joan's two younger brothers were more or less contemporary with Tommy and George. The Hallward family and Miss Verschoyle were also among the friends of those early years at "Grattons".

The Simpsons lived in a very nice old house in Dunsfold with a big barn. Mr. Simpson was a retired clergyman. His eldest child, Joan, was a very lively nurse in India and became a very good friend of Violet's. There was a younger daughter Doris, and the eldest son, George was in the navy and eventually became a submariner. He befriended his namesake George and on one occasion took him in his submarine on an exercise. Ralph Simpson, another son, became a teacher at Tavistock (Devon) for all his life. The Simpson family had a good influence on the Grimshaws. Eventually he bought the house below Violet's house at Garth on Longdown outside Guildford. They used to go frequently on naturalist expeditions in the local forests and woods and on one occasion George Simpson climbing up a great tree to get eggs from a magpies nest - he brought the eggs down in his mouth. The Grimshaw love as a family for the natural world was greatly influenced by the Simpsons. Their wonderful large home had two staircases – and the children had a lot of fun there playing "hide and seek" and "murder".

Violet's eldest sister Ella must have moved to England soon after the war, though she had been helping with the administration of hospitals in Egypt during the war. She was a great stand by. Others who often visited were Cecil's sisters Emma and Gladys.

Violet was a keen gardener and there were two herbaceous borders in front of the house on either side of a broad gravel walk leading down to a pond. David can vaguely remember he and his mother putting little notes in the flowers for the fairies - no doubt part of a program of developing the imagination and keeping him out of mischief. On one occasion, it is reliably reported that David fell into the lily pond and was saved from drowning by the furry coat he was wearing which seems to have acted as some sort of life jacket! Violet gave a lot of time to David in those early years which was no doubt good therapy for her.

There were trips in the pony trap to Cranleigh (4 miles) and Godalming (6 miles) to the dentist, for photography sessions, shopping and such like. There was a steep hill on the way into the latter town and they all had to get out and walk up it. When they went into Guildford the local market town (10 miles) the trap was left at "The Lion Hotel" and they had exciting meals at the "Astolat Cafe".

One feature of the garden at "Grattons" was a leveled area underneath a large spreading oak tree. Violet had had it made during the very hot summer of 1916 so they could have all our meals outside. This was the scene of many happy tea parties that included strawberries and cream or raspberries when in season. The main hazards were wasps and caterpillars that descended on long threads from the branches.

Violet was a great entertainer and always seemed to have friends around. Uncle O'Donnell and his wife Nea, and daughters Ruth and Mimi were often present on these occasions. There were games of tennis and croquet. Uncle O'Donnell was very good with his hands and made lots of useful items for the family, nesting boxes for the tits, and a covered bird table, fIre screens and the like. Violet was very fond of birds and loved watching the tits hanging from bits of fat and upturned coconuts.

One famous party was given by Chiefs Black Eagle (David Grimshaw) and Brown Bear (Harcourt Merritt). Invitations went out to all the surrounding braves on brown paper singed round the edges to resemble pieces of bark. They all had feathered headdresses and beaded outfits - much of it made by Violet with great imagination. She was very resourceful when it came to anything of this kind. They had a big bonfire, fireworks, potatoes baked in the embers and much merriment. It was all part of Violet's home making skill. She encouraged all sorts of fun and activities around the home, including charades and dumb-crambo.

They were happy days. George had a happy time in his words *"from my point of view, as a child there is no reason you wouldn't be happy unless someone was bullying you or beating you or knocking you around or something. We had a very happy time. Tommy was the wild one and I was the sort of go between. Tommy used to go off - Violet used to lock Tommy up in his bedroom, and while he was supposed to be in there he could always climb out of any room in the house. Both boys could.*

I don't know if I admired him, but I was his sort of little fag. He would escape and I would see him beckoning me from the orchard and I would get my instructions to go and steal some bread and food from the larder and join him and off we would go to the woods".

David was too small, he was still in the pram. Life just developed. They had a nanny, Milly, who was the wheelwright's daughter, and so George and his brothers were always going up to the wheelwright's shop with her; she'd take the boys there to see her parents. It was very interesting really. George used to spend hours watching him put iron collars on cartwheels and things like that.

Tommy went off to boarding school in Portsmouth (the same one that his father had attended); he hated it and was taken away and eventually ended up at Boxgrove (near Guildford). Tommy and George both went there, partly because Uncle

O'Donnell was quite close and he could keep an eye on them.

George went to Boxgrove, when he was about eight, just as the War ended, Tommy was already there. He was there at the time of the terrible influenza epidemic, there was only one boy in the whole school who hadn't get influenza - Charles Buckley, George remembered that he used to come round and read stories to them.

Violet was a very, very, adventurous and inventive woman, if she had been a man she would have been an entrepreneur. She used to get, the headmaster (who was known as Uncle Buftie, he was a Cauldwell from the Cauldwell Paper Mills in Scotland), to come out with a whole lot of boys for picnics at Grattons, so there was quite a close link with home.
Uncle Buftie had a Ford, a limousine, it was an upright thing with running boards. Uncle O'Donnell kept Violet in cars, if anything went wrong, the whole garage staff turned up on his instructions to put it right.

Violet was a very lively lady. She was very good at tennis

Boxgrove Preparatory School, Guildford. Ist XI Cricket team. George - front row left. Tommy (captain) center row, center

and other games. She was marvelous at nosing out people who had children of the same age. In those days there was the system where one called on people and left ones card and then if they wanted to they would invite you back, or if one happened to meet them somewhere they would probably invite one to stay for tea or a drink. She used to spot families like the Rogersons - Michael Rogerson was at Marlborough School, and was the same age as George (they remained friends for life). There was another family, the Lampsons, and there were all sorts of families around the district and they all had children. Violet used to organise, in the holidays, pitch hockey parties and hockey matches on the common.

Violet was ably assisted at this time by Ethel Sadler, who came to as a governess for David and in considerable measure as companion to Violet. Miss Sadler came from the family of Major Norton, who had died in one of the first attempts to conquer Mt. Everest, which gave her a certain prestige in the children's eyes. She also understood the problems of a widow trying to bring up her family on her own. She was, a marvelous teacher and managed by her enthusiasm to invest everything from "Reading without tears", to sums, nature study and visits to Museums with colour and interest.

Violet made friends with a Mrs. Poe, also a widow, who had a town house in Kensington Court, opposite Kensington Gardens in London. She had a daughter called Bunny. They stayed at Grattons in the summer and Violet and family stayed with them in the winter. It was whilst staying with her in London that Miss Sadler and David visited most of the famous museums.

Another mainstay of the family was Emily Miles, who came to in March 1924, as cook housekeeper. She soon became very much part of the family, knitting stockings and sweaters, washing clothes that had got covered with mud while beagling, or paper-chasing, or birds nesting or whatever. Nothing was too much trouble, quite apart from providing marvelous meals.

Violet had quite a battle to make ends meet at that period.

Tommy and George were fortunately accepted on the Foundation at Wellington. The school had been founded to educate the sons of officers killed in the campaigns of the Duke of Wellington, and a considerable capital sum had been subscribed in order to subsidize those less well off. Violet's widow's pension was £168 per year, and she received an allowance from her father, but more was required. So with her usual inventiveness she made contact with a New Zealand family whose sons went to school at Clifton College and needed a home for the holidays. No chance of getting back to New Zealand in those days, when the sea journey took six weeks! And so the association with the Merritt family began. H. (Harry) T. Merritt was a timber merchant in Auckland evidently in a fairly large way. Both he and his wife, Auntie Bessie, were of Scottish extraction. Chisholm the eldest boy was contemporary with Tommy, Roy with George, and Harcourt was about a year older than David. So they were a large and lively household in the holidays, but Violet managed to devise a busy program of tennis tournaments, hockey matches and running with the beagles to keep them all occupied. Emily was assisted in the holidays by a temporary 'parlour maid'.

There were several families of about the same age in the neighbourhood. Violet played bridge with the parents as well as tennis. Violet played a good game of tennis as is evidenced by the number of tournaments in which she took part all over the area, recorded in her diaries. The children played tennis, went for picnics on the river and organised paper chases and hockey matches. Graham and Mary were the children of Ernest H. Shepherd, the illustrator of A.A. Milne's "Winnie the Pooh" and "Now we are six". Then there was the Prescott family of five boys and two girls.. Their father was President of the Rugby Union Association, and they were all keen followers of the game and some of them excellent players too. Tony captained the England side, and Robin the Army side later on.

Violet used to go calling on any suitable family with boys and girls of our age, for example the Rogersons. Her Visitors Book (really "callers" book) shows how far and wide she cast her net! She was very particular about our contacts and always inspected the boys Dance Programs to see that they had "done their duty" and danced with the less popular girls as well as our favourites! One winter Ernest Shepherd produced A.A. Milnes "Make Believe". There were a good many pirates required so roles were found for most of them!

On Sundays the family all trooped off to the 13th Century Church of St Mary and All Saints. It boasted a fine peel of bells and they could hear them across the fields from home. When the weather was fine and the ground dry they went across the fields at the bottom of the garden. Sometimes they took the chance of a stroll in the woods, before returning for Sunday lunch. This was not encouraged by the local gamekeeper, but their expeditions seldom coincided with his! They used to be impressed by his larders which contained stoats and jays and other predators of the pheasants he was rearing for the Squire's shooting parties. There were lots of birds nests in the trees and hedgerows. David has quite a vivid memory of Violet going off on her own to Holy Communion in a long skirted costume in dark green and navy and wide brimmed hat and gloves of course! Early pictures of the Alderson family show them to have had considerable dress sense and Violet was always very well turned out. She had a white bound Prayer Book with a silver cross on it.

"Grattons" had five bedrooms, one of which was the maid's room, so it is difficult to imagine how they all fitted in. In the summer time they used to sleep under canvas in the garden. Violet's diaries showed her life divided between holidays when everything revolved around her boys, and term time when she went to bridge and tennis parties, made expeditions to London to theatres and concerts, and visits to family and friends.

Three other examples of Violet's resourcefulness and planning come to mind. In 1921 the family acquired its first car, a 'Tin Lizzie'! a T Model Ford with a two man hood and side curtains and paraffin oil side lights, the headlights were electric. About the same time they had a Delco electricity generating set installed - a great improvement on the smoky paraffin lights that had been used till then. And finally Violet had the sides of the hay barn filled in to make a marvelous playroom for the boys. Tommy and George had a large collection of Meccano and model trains.

George went to Boxgrove Preparatory School when he was 8 and left at 13. He then went to Wellington College. Wellington was chosen simply because it had a foundation, and children of officers who had been killed in the War only paid £12 a term. Tommy preceded George to Wellington by 2 years going there in 1921, but he was always revolutionary. He didn't work, he didn't want to work really. George very soon caught up with him in work. He was 3 years older than George but he was still in a lower class.

They ended up in the same form. Tommy eventually left early because he didn't like the discipline; he wouldn't tolerate any discipline at all. He was the sort of man who if he had actually become a soldier would have been a real fighter. He'd would have probably won the VC or some other medal of valor! Against all rules and regulations at the school, he used to keep wild birds and other creatures down at the laundry. The school had its own laundry which was just outside the immediate precinct, down the hill. Tommy had an owl there at one time and a couple of jackdaws, and he used to go there and feed them. It was out of bounds, but the staff at the laundry must have cooperated. It all went very well until Violet came along and didn't realise it was wrong and blew the gaffe on it.

Tommy was not very interested in sports. He was always in trouble. George was the good boy, and must have been most annoying, it must have driven Tommy crazy, but George applied himself to his work and to sports and anything else that passed in front of him.

"I just followed my nose so to speak and my nose led in that direction, I don't know why. I have often thought about it and tried to see how it happened. I think it was that Tommy was the wild one and when David was on the way Violet needed a lot of support and I was the sort of blue eyed boy who was always sitting on her lap or at her knees listening to stories

she would read and things like that, and I was just brought up by women all my life. Later on in life, when she was trying to make ends meet, she had three boys from New Zealand, almost exactly the same age as the three Grimshaw boys. They were all at Clifton, and Violet used to come home and would made an awful fuss about me and, I don't know, I just became a woman's boy. I suppose that's why I still get on better with women than I do with men, I don't know whether that is anything to do with it. I was rather dependent and kept the law".

"I was always on the side of the law, therefore the law was pleased with you and supported one. I don't think that sort of leadership is necessarily the best. Tommy would have been a much better leader at war than I ever would have been I am sure, because he was wild and he'd do anything.

He would have to have been a Chindit or something like that or in the SAS I am sure he would not have been a square basher. But I don't think that its always that creditable to be on the side of the law and be applying oneself and enjoying being successful.

I did not make many friends at Wellington. Probably because being an authority (Head of School, Captain of most of the sports teams) in school in a way isolates you. The one person I did make friends with went into the Air Force and got killed in Norway, he was called Reggie Elsmie. But otherwise I don't think I did make a lot of chums really, I was too occupied playing sports."

In July 1924 Tommy left Wellington. The early part of the summer had seen a busy round of tennis, garden parties and fetes, interspersed with visits to Wellington and days when Tommy and George could get home for the day, sometimes bringing friends. After Tommy and George came home the pace hotted up; hardly a day passed without a tennis or cricket match somewhere. There were also picnics and several visits to Violet's brother Uncle Bertie Alderson and Aunt Mabel at Burwash in Sussex.

Then came the Christmas holidays with the return of the Merritt family, George and David from various schools, and a hectic round of parties, dances, beagling and rehearsals for the play produced by Ernest Shepherd of "Winnie the Pooh" fame.

Towards the end of those holidays Violet rented a house in Seaview, Isle of Wight for a fortnight. They traveled there by the paddle-steamer from Portsmouth to Ryde. They had by this time acquired a sailing boat. This must have been during a previous summer holidays which were spent at Mrs. Poe's cottage at Fishbourne, then a quiet little village. It has since become the terminal for the ferry service from Portsmouth, which replaced the paddle steamers. The boat had been brought round from its winter quarters at the top of Wootton Creek and left on a mooring in the bay, where it was riding happily when they arrived. The next morning they were down at the jetty early, but there was nothing to be seen of the boat. Then they spotted the small pennant at the top of the mast flying just above the water! There followed a memorable salvage operation watched by a large crowd of holiday makers. The boat was hauled up on the beach, re-caulked, re-launched and provided good sport for the rest of our stay. It was a very seaworthy and safe half-decker. She was called "Blue Bird".

Around this time it became clear that the daily motor-bike ride in and out of Guildford to get the train to London was proving too tiring for Tommy, and Violet began to look around for a home in Guildford.

An unusual event was the arrival of the stunningly beautiful Alderson cousin, Irene. This triggered a round of dances including a dance that Violet and sons arranged in the village Hall.

In 1926 Grattons was sold to Miss Arbuthnot on Jan 25th - it fetched $3,610 (in 2004 it was sold for £1,500,000). Violet then traveled abroad.

During her absence abroad or possibly before she had left she had purchased an acre of land on the top of a ridge on the

Sailing Blue Bird at Seaview Isle of Wight 1927. Tommy, George and David with Michael Rogerson, George's life long friend.

south side of Guildford. It had a superb view of the Chantry Woods, St. Martha's, the old pilgrim church and the Surrey Hills beyond. It was on Longdown Road, at that time just a gravel track, and had been part of the Godwin-Austen estates. A week after her return she was up there 'setting a man to work' and 'carting laurels' to establish protective hedges. Some of them dug up from "Grattons". Violet moved out of "Grattons" on June 7th 1926, and spent the night with her old friends the Simpsons in the village.

Another spell at Seaview, and then the Autumn term for George and David. Tommy and George must have been based with

Aunt Ella at this time, as indeed they all were. She had a home called "Braeside" on the Hogs Back, near Farnham.

For the Christmas holidays that year Violet had rented a house at the corner of Waterden Road and Epsom Road in Guildford. There were various festivities. The Merritt boys were still with them. They all had 'flu' and Violet had to get a nurse in to look after them. She was a rather fearsome lady who smoked like a chimney!

Tommy had by this time joined the Territorial Army and Violet had noted December 31st, as the Territorial Ball. Tommy also played for the Guildford R.F.C. at that time. Violet's father died in December 1926. On Feb 19th 1927 she moved into the new house she had built at Longdown Road. She named it "Garth".

Garth, Longdown, Guildford. Circa 1931 (tennis court on left)

The early months of 1927 must have been a very busy time with much settling in to do. The garden at Longdown Road had been basically landscaped. The area for the ten-

St. Martha's on the Pilgrim Way, viewed from Garth. In its churchyard are buried Tommy (1942) and Violet (1943), and George Grimshaw and Nancy Gilliat were married (November 30th 1937)

Page 71

nis court and herbaceous borders had been leveled. Steps had been built from this area up to a terrace, in the centre of which was a lily pond. A dry brick wall divided this area from a higher terrace surrounding the house itself, and a broad flight of steps led from the lily pond level to the porch in the centre of the house. But all this had to be cultivated and prepared and then planted, with roses, shrubs, bulbs and rock plants. Violet was always very fond of rock roses, possibly because rock roses grew wild on Gallipoli, and maybe there was an association with Cecil in her fondness for these plants. Cecil was also very fond of dog roses, the wild briars of the hedgerows.

The move to Guildford brought them into closer and more constant touch with the Gilliat family who lived in Merrow. There were three boys and three girls, the elder ones being keen tennis players, and George soon got included in their games.

Soon after occupying Garth another house was completed lower down the hill. It seemed that the view towards St. Martha's - that meant so much to the family - would soon be spoiled by other 'hideous' houses. It is perhaps a tribute to Violet's entrepreneurial skills that she promptly negotiated the purchase of the block of land in front of Garth and proceeded to build a house on one corner of it. The house was designed with a low roof line, and was barely visible behind the embankment on which the Garth tennis court was laid. The house was sub-

Garth, Sunken Garden circa 1931, still there in 2006. Chantry woods in background

Garth, Longdown, Guildford. Circa 2006 (tennis court on left)

sequently sold to the Simpson family from Dunsfold, with a caveat in the title deed that nothing could be built on the land in the Garth line of view of St. Martha's. It was said that no one but good friends like the Simpsons would have bought it on those conditions!

Tennis party at Garth, Violet at center with Benbow, the family bull terrier to the right.

On December 1st, Violet apparently lunched with the Duchess of Wellington. Possibly an occasion connected with Wellington College, though it could have been a Red Cross occasion as Aunt Emma, who had been awarded their Medal of Merit, came to stay immediately afterwards. Later she went to see

Ruth Draper with (Mrs.) Bessie Merritt.

George – the young man

The new year, 1928, started with all the usual family activities of the Christmas holidays. George, however, went to Switzerland to an O.C.U. (Officers Christian Union) Winter Sports House Party, no doubt invited by the Gilliat family. This was the beginning of big changes in the family life.

George: *"Another factor that came into my life was this question of being a Christian. One of the families Violet picked up was the Gilliat family and through them we got introduced to the Officers Christian Union and whilst I was still at Wellington. I went out to the Officers' Christian Union Winter Sports in Switzerland and we had talks every morning on the challenge to give one's life to Christ, and I did. That would have made you be on the side of the law. It's extraordinary how it had an adverse effect on my relationships. I suppose I got rather critical in a way of people who weren't Christian or who didn't pray. Wellington wasn't a Christian foundation necessarily although it was a Church of England foundation, very much so. I used to go to communion and I was confirmed incidentally at my prep school, Boxgrove. I was confirmed by the romantic Bishop of the Arctic. He was the father of one of the staff. The Headmaster gave me a copy of Daily Life when I was confirmed and I have read Daily Life all my life. I went to chapel and things like that. I must have been maddeningly goody goody in a way."*

The O.C.U. was a Union of Christian Officers with a distinct evangelical tradition - Its members were always encouraging young men destined for the armed services to join and face the challenge of living for and witnessing to the Lord Jesus Christ as a personal Saviour. Wives and sisters who joined as Associates were the logistical support group organising house parties, etc, and maintaining regular prayer groups. Hence George and David's participation and later Violet's. The Gilliat and Lankester families were very active associates.

George who was by this time Head Boy at Wellington and Captain of the Rugby XV and the Hockey XI, went back to college.

That summer saw their first camp at West Wittering on the eastern head of Chichester Harbour. Joan Simpson was with them. It became their favourite seaside holiday spot until the Schneider Trophy Race was flown in the area in September 1929 and it became too crowded and they moved to Itchenor. The Schneider Trophy was won that year by Squadron Leader Orlebar flying a Napier Supermarine - the prototype of the famous Hurricanes and Spitfires. There were further picnics at Wittering and in the Chantry Wood, on one of which 5 I/2

George - center sitting - Captain of Rugby at Wellington College

lbs of blackberries were picked (blackberry picking was always a Grimshaw tradition in September and coincided with George's birthday!).

In September 1928, George went back to Wellington for his last term and David went with him for his first! He remembers

Page 75

vividly standing with George in the doorway to the long dormitory, the Murray. It was George's privilege not to wear a cap, but for a 'squealer' like David not to, was a heinous crime. Somehow David had arrived without one. George let out a great bellow and boys came running from all sides. He ordered one of them to find David a cap, which was placed on David's head and decorum was restored! It was a very crumpled and inky affair and was soon replaced by a clean one from the school shop! George took pride in improving the tuckshop - known as "Grubbies" - he was responsible for it moving from just a shop selling food to one that included sports gear and other equipment. He was also responsible for the introduction of field hockey as a sport, one that he excelled at. George took the Army Exam in November giving him entry to the Royal Military Academy, Woolwich, which he entered on February 1st, 1929.

George as an Army cadet whilst at Wellington College with Benbow

Family life went on much as usual. Violet planned and built a squash court on the Simpsons property, sharing the expense with them and the family of Ernest Shepherd who by this time had moved from Shamley Green and built next door to them at Longdown Road. The present owner wrote in 'The Surrey Advertiser' in 1989 about Ernest Shepherd's house in Longdown Road, and referred to "his friend Mrs.. Grimshaw who introduced him to the site". The Merritt family were still with them. Chisholm got his commission from the Royal Military College, Sandhurst and left for overseas in March 1929. Auntie Bessie, Roy, Harcourt, Violet and David went for a holiday to St. Lunaire in Normandy in August of that year. Violet played much bridge that autumn.

On Boxing Day 1929 George and David went to Switzerland with the Gilliats and Lankesters to another O.C.U. gathering organised by Brigadier David Foster. Robin Lankester was about David's age and they had become good friends. He slept on the luggage rack!.

Years later Robin was to recall for his memories of Violet. *"Violet - she was a delightful, dynamic creature! She never did anything by halves and of course she shouldered the heavy responsibility of bringing up the family on her own. I know that Violet had a great rapport with my mother, and had fierce debates, first about British Israel and the pyramids, and later Moral Rearmament (MRA) - and although we never agreed altogether about that we never lost contact and maintained the dialogue with her and with Bish (Aunt Ella's friend). Also Violet, in addition to making the lovely garden at Garth showed great enterprise in building those houses at Leatherhead. (only one in point of fact). She was always so kind to me in the days when you and I spent most of our holidays together, and of course her wild driving with one arm on the wheel and the other gesticulating to emphasize a point or to point out some feature of the South Downs were so characteristic of her - also picnics at the Helmet and Camping in your caravan at Wittering. And of course she built up a strong coterie of friends on Longdown - the Holdens, Simpsons, Shepherds and Turners - that we all enjoyed".*

George was not part of the wild "club" rugby crowd. *"I always though that was all wrong. It wasn't a good influence in my life really. From that day on I never went to a dance, although I loved going to holiday dances and such things with all the young people and from that day we weren't allowed to go to theatres. It was a terribly Plymouth Brethren form of Christianity. If you were in the crowd it was alright but once you were outside the crowd - you had to make a stand. Anything that was wrong you had to make a stand against you see. It was an extreme evangelical, and in some ways in retrospect it was my religion that cut me off from family."*

"Some people, the best people, are Christians that can get on with people outside, they seem to cross the barrier and have fun with people outside. I was able to have lots of sporting fun, I played in tennis tournaments and hockey matches in the holidays and all that sort of thing, but the moment it was over - I would never go to the pub with the Rugby players. They knew that, so one was an outsider. In a way it still goes on now. It's very interesting, I notice even here in Ringmore, somehow or another the men aren't comfortable with me. I am not really comfortable with them. This is something that is implanted in me. I mean if they want to be friendly I am perfectly comfortable with them."

George was for all his life handicapped by two things, not being able to remember people or remember their names. At Wellington he was given a list of all the boys at the school and various rules and regulations and was supposed to learn the whole lot of them – he managed to do this for his own House - Murray – and that was all. When he went to Wellington as a new boy he was put through all sorts of tests. Violet had never taught him any "parlour tricks" or songs. He couldn't sing a note. He had never learned any poetry or any songs or anything, He was never been able to. The only things he learned were some of the prayers that he had said so often. When he went to Wellington, every new boy had to stand up in the middle of the House and sing a song. He couldn't do it and eventually he just about managed to make some "awful mess" of the National Anthem and that's all. He remembers feeling ashamed of himself. If he had been brought up by his father, it would have been different. He was never able to entertain anybody, even at an old age. He considered it one of the weak spots in his make-up. But at sports, of course, he was able to dominate.

He worked hard at sports and was fitter than most boys; He would win the cross-country races. He got in the first Rugby XV at a very young age (fifteen) and was there for 3 years. He was in the scrum – loose forward. He was quite big but wasn't very heavy. He was Captain for two years, then he played for England School Boys against the Scotland School Boys. He was also Captain of field hockey and athletics, and regularly won the Fives competition with his friend Reggie Elves. At Wellington he ended up as Head Boy and won the King's Medal.

He wrecked his knee when skiing, and as a result always had a weakness there, that was difficult. It troubled him all his life - he just put up with it.

George – A Soldier with Promise

After leaving Wellington George entered "The Shop" in 1929. The Royal Military Academy, Woolwich (1741-1939). During the mid-eighteenth century the expansion of the British interests aboard and in particular the protection of those interests highlighted to the Board of Ordnance the need for adequately trained officers competent to carry out those responsibilities, so in 1741 the Royal Military Academy, Woolwich (The Shop) was created to meet those training needs for "instructing the people of its Military branch to form good Officers of Artillery and perfect Engineers".

The Royal Military Academy (RMA) provided the high level of scientific education required by the Artillery (nicked named The Gunners) and Engineers (nicked named The Sappers), while at the same time ensuring that their officers had the same quality of military training as those serving in the Line. The cadets were referred to as 'gentleman cadets' and were only granted their commission after completing the course. On passing out from the Academy, the new officers were placed in order of merit. Promotion within the Corps was by seniority, not by purchase. This was a great incentive to study. A difference of one or two places in the final order of merit at the RMA could result in many years difference in later promotion, as the career pyramid narrowed in the higher ranks.

The Shop produced artillery officers (the Gunners}, engineers (the Sappers) and the Signals. George was there for about 18 months. In 1930 he won the Tombs memorial Prize (1877-1939) for the best qualified cadet commissioned into The Royal Artillery; also the Earl Roberts Memorial Prize in 1931 for the youngest officer most deserving on the grounds of efficiency and character during his cadetship at the Royal Military Academy (RMA). He was awarded the Sword of Honour at the passing out parade at The Shop for the best overall Officer Cadet.

He says that at that time he ran out of steam. *"I think I had too much responsibility when I was young, so I didn't particularly want it later. Interestingly it was predicted at both school and The Shop that he would be head of the Army or Navy. It was felt that he ought to have done but he didn't. He preferred to be head of a family. Its rather interesting really because when I read these obituaries of people who have gone on ahead after World War II. I just realise that I had no ambitions for that at all, I was entirely satisfied with my own family. It was very selfish, but I just felt that the family and the home mattered much more than any of these other things really. That sort of ambition often drives an individual but is tough on the family. The good Lord made me a family man and later sent me off to Africa as part of the Church Missionary Society".*

After the Shop he went to Larkhill on Salisbury Plain, to a Junior Officer's Course. *"When we left the Shop we became officers, Second Lieutenant, and we got a Commission from the King (George V). He was high enough up on the Passing Out list (third), he could have had anything he wanted. He could have been an Engineer or a Signals or Gunner. You had to be high up to get into the Engineers, there weren't many officers required. He could have become an Engineer but the Gunners sounded a little more exciting. There is a the little ditty - Gunners are poor, proud and prejudiced, Sappers are mad, married and Methodists"*

The Gunners appealed to him because in those days they had horses - the Gunners were the Royal Horse Artillery. There was no mechanisation in those days - horses pulled the guns. Officers were allocated horses to go hunting - twice a week. He went to Whittington barracks (near Lichfield) and eventually joined the Regiment. He had a batman and a groom and went fox hunting. The Army doesn't do that now - they don't fox hunt. It was great fun - galloping across country and hoping not to fall off and break one's neck - It was all part of the test of valour. Fox hunting on horses was said in those days to be good for ones character, and it requires courage and determination. It also develops the eye for the terrain and potential routes for the guns. When hunting he wore a top hat, tail coat, yellow waistcoat and top boots – no hard hats in those days!

It was all great fun, nobody was thinking of war. It was an exciting future for a young man.

The Larkhill course was very serious, teaching real gunnery. At the Shop it was all basics, military life, discipline, and a certain amount of military history, military law etc. They learned all this at the Shop, as well as strategy and tactics. At Larkhill he learned about gunnery, how to operate the artillery and how to fire the guns. There were no ear muffs in those days. The guns were all 18 pounder field guns, which had been developed from the original 13 pounders. As officers they were treated like ordinary gunners. They had to man the gun themselves; they did everything, one day he was the sergeant in charge of a gun, another day the battery commander; he had to learn it all. Then there was the observation, questions on Ops, Observation Posts, how to fire the guns and what commands were sent to the guns. The course lasted about nine months.

At that time he was courting Barbara Gilliat (living at Levlys Dene, near Guildford), and he used to go off on his motorbike to visit her. He had an old AGS that he bought for £5. He would rush up to Levyls Dene whenever he had a chance. He met Barbara through tennis parties. He used to ride back absolutely frozen in the winter - it was so cold and wet on a motorbike, but he had a marvelous batman who always left a roaring great fire; the officers were in wooden huts which were temporary buildings really. They were good days.

Levyls Dene, Merrow, Guildford. The home of Algernon and Marjorie Gilliat whose daughters Barbara and Nancy were to marry George

He started courting Barbara when he was at Larkhill. Then he was posted to a battery in Borden, near Aldershot and very soon learned that the Regiment was to set off for India. After a few months, still a bachelor, he was posted to India.

2nd Lt George Grimshaw – Before the War in India (1931-1937)

In September 1931 the 6th Brigade Royal Artillery was to go to Lucknow located in India's United Provinces. They traveled by sea. It was a great trip, it took weeks to get there. This was his first real experience of going abroad, as before that he had only been to Switzerland, for winter sports. The Summer Series - were special troop ships designed for troops, and for the ranks it was a pretty miserable, they all slept in hammocks down below. As an officer, 2nd Lt. George Grimshaw had a cabin on the higher decks.

They sailed via the Suez Canal whiling away the time, playing bridge or deck games. There was a canvas swimming bath strung up on deck that they dipped themselves in. He remember spending hours on deck just talking to people. Then of course there were people from other regiments - there were Ghurka officers, Infantry officers, and there were other assorted officers and their families. There were a lot of young girls going to India to look for husbands – they were known as the "Fishing Fleet"!

They arrived in Bombay (Mumbai) and the troop ship was surrounded by people trying to lend them money and old servants greeting people who were returning. It was always a great occasion when troop ships arrived. On arrival they took the train. In those days the train has the sort of right of way. It would stop on request to get water for shaving and then the old security guard says go on - regardless of timetables. George considered himself lucky to arrive in India at tail end of the Raj when English people were really respected and had a sort of right of passage wherever they went. It was beginning to change a bit before, but being part of the army the change was less noticeable, no doubt the civilian administration noticed it more.

The train journey took 2 or 3 days. The engines were coal burning, lots of dust, and George's bearer would climb along the roof of the carriages to get boiling water for making tea and shaving. Trains moved very slowly in those days!. In India many trains had people sitting on the carriage roofs. It was always interesting to see the countryside because most of them had never been to India before. The general impression was a landscape that was fairly flat, dry and dusty, not much greenery. At the stations lots of little boys begging - tapping their tummies to show they wanted food. It was all so new to these young soldiers from far away green England. *"One tended to be a sort of globule moving through space, you were a sort of group moving through the countryside without any contact with it at all really".* In those days the Englishman expected to be held in respect wherever he went. It helped develop self confidence, and they needed that.

Lucknow is in United Province on the Gomati River some 250 miles south east of Delhi, and was his first posting in India. He arrived there in 1931 at the age of 21. George had friends from the Shop - Alistair Mitchell was his great friend. He went off in a different regiment, Horse Artillery. George was never one for deep friendships with men, He didn't know why, perhaps because he was brought up by women the whole time. When he got, to Lucknow, he was billeted in the house of his battery captain, because he had a spare room and was a bachelor.

They arrived at the cantonment - almost entirely army – with all the different regiments herded together in one great area out side the town of Lucknow. It was very hot. Except for some of the older men none of them had experienced this sort of weather. The troops settled in comfortably and were reasonably happy. George was put in charge of organising Christmas day events. He found a contractor with a camel who brought in Father Christmas.

There was a lot of sport going on all the time - horse racing, tennis, squash and hockey. He played at various clubs. The regiment had a coach and four and nobody, except the Colonel who enjoyed driving it, wanted it. George enjoyed driving it, and used to drive it to the club, a groom held the horses whilst he played tennis. Eventually he took it with him to camp and he drove it to the Delhi Horse Show (250 miles) - some feat in those days. It was a marathon drive but he did it just because it happened to be there. He was rather keen on the practice camp in Delhi. Once a year they went into camp and fired the guns - always good fun.

He always had lots of men (bearers) around to look after him. His was a good man - a Muslim - very nice chap. When he subsequently returned to India after his leave, with a wife (Barbara), the bearer left as he wouldn't work with a woman.

Pig sticking was the other activity - they would put the horses on the train and go with them to the Terai (plains along the foothills of the Himalayas. They rode through the country and

George was an active sportsman in India, polo plaryer, pigsticker and hunter

chased wild pigs with the object of spearing. Rather like fox hunting except that the pig was killed with a spear. It was quite dangerous because whilst galloping across the country side after the pig, one couldn't see where one was going. Plenty of adrenalin! After the British left India nearly all the pigs got slaughtered. They camped in one of those great "baghs" as they were called, in a clearing in a forest of mango trees.

The role of the army was security and aid to civil peace. There was a certain amount of action up on the North West Frontier. There was always something going on up there because of the competition between Russia and Britain and other countries. and the army would patrol this remote and dangerous area. The army's main role was to support the political and civil administration as needed, apart from that it was part of the colonial strategic reserve. India was divided up into states. Lucknow was in the United Provinces and there was a governor, a British governor - they were all British in those days. The Maharajas were in their own states. They had their own armies. The Maharajas had a lot of independence but they were very much under the rule of the British. The relationships with them were generally good. George often used participate in pig sticking, hunting and polo tournaments on the maharajas estates. The Maharaja of Mysore was a great polo player. He used to pitch a wonderful camp and they would all go and stay there.

When he first went out to India as a bachelor he happened to get to know a man who turned out to be the boyfriend and future husband, of the daughter of the Governor of Rawlapindi. The second Christmas he was in India, he was sent an invitation from the Governor to go on a "Gooming" Christmas holiday. Gooming is trailing round the forest on four or five elephants, trying to find a tiger. He thought this was a bit odd, until he discovered on arrival that the daughter and her boyfriend had invited a friend of hers, and George was invited to share an elephant with the young woman. He would have preferred to shoot on his own!

Nothing came of it but it went on all that Christmas week. Many years later when George was chairman of the Lee Abbey Committee, a young man came up to him and said *"Do you remember so-and-so in India"*. It meant absolutely nothing to him, as he had forgotten all about this episode and he said, *"well as a matter of fact I don't think I do"*, and he said *"well you spent quite a long time on an elephant with a young lady"* and I said *"oh yes, I did, why?"* Well, he said, *"she is my mother"*.

Overall he had quite a profitable time, he shot a bear when he was up on a hide in a tree. They used to go with the elephants and some time during the day they were put up on trees, and the beaters that were provided would beat the forest and he was just lucky that during one of the beats a bear trundled underneath his hide and he shot him. He also stalked antelope.

He used to go out early in the morning before anyone else was up, on another occasion he got a crocodile and a leopard. He sent the skins to a taxidermist for mounting. He had the bear and the leopard for a long time, finally giving the leopard to the base drummer in Harry Grimshaw's regiment (the latter was in Kenya during the Mau Mau time - 1950s) .

He was in Lucknow for three years - as a bachelor - then he went back to England on leave in the Spring of 1934. On arrival he and Barbara Gilliat got engaged, and later married on July 28th at St John's church in Merrow. Levys Dene was in Merrow, a couple of miles east of Guildford on the edge of the south downs.

George had 6 months leave, and then the newly married couple returned to Lucknow for about a year. He was then posted to Bangalore (south India on the Deccan Plateau). He went down there to be part of the training cadre for the first Indian field artillery. Because of the Indian Mutiny, the Indians were not allowed field artillery as there was always the fear that there might be another mutiny. Now however they were training the Indians towards the day when they would

George married Barbara Gilliat on July 28th 1934

have their own field artillery. They had a regiment in Bangalore, each with four batteries, each with a different group of Indians, some Punjabis, Murathis, all from different parts of India. They had never been trained for field artillery. They had been manning mountain light artillery up in the North West Frontier - all carried on pack mules - but they had not been allowed to have any field guns or any other sort of heavy artillery.

Being at higher altitude, Bangalore was much cooler. There were more married people there. Most were doing the same thing there, training the Indians. When he first went to India he was in a British unit, comprising all British except the servants, but in Bangalore it was an Indian regiment - they were all Indian except the officers and a few NCOs and who were seconded to it. Army life was a bit more serious, they had to train these chaps to be prepared to take senior positions when the Indian Army expanded. It was a good time.

George sailing on a Lake near Bangalore, India

There were three Indian Officers who had been through Woolwich, the Shop. One very nice man was Kamaramonggalun, know as "K", whose father was a republican politician. K used to come over quite a lot and play with Gillian (George's eldest daughter born in Bangalore on June 9th 1935) when she was tiny. His father was an ardent anti-English politician. Another was Gayani, a Sikh. He did very well - he was a gunner during the war in the Indian Army. Later he was commanding the U.N. troops in Cyprus.

In Bangalore George started sailing again. They were not far from some lakes, and had some boats called snipes, they were very simple boats to build. The artificers built them. They were quite good, though a bit rough and the sails were flat having been made by the local tailor. Barbara was never in a state to sail, she was pregnant at the beginning with Gillian but she used to come and watch.

They had a well staffed house in those days - a total of 13! including 2 butlers (bearers), a cook, an Ayha (nurse maid), a gardener, a sweeper, 2 or 3 syces (grooms), the latter for the polo ponies. They had a man to drive the car - they got hold of an old Citreon motor car that they used to go to the Nilgiri hills. The latter are 120 miles south west of Bangalore on the Kerala border part of India's Western Ghats. It was a great place for people to go on leave, as it was a beautiful area. They used to go trout fishing and take the baby, Gillian, they would borrow somebody's house.

Then tragedy struck for George. On September 13th 1936, Barbara died of hemorrhage giving birth to their second child. She was buried next day in the Christian cemetery at Bangalore. Strangely enough her cousin, Joyce Gilliat, slightly younger than Barbara, and daughter of Walter Gilliat, the great footballer educated at Charterhouse, died in exactly the same way.

It was a difficult time, fortunately they had a marvelous ayha who looked after Gillian. Violet came out, supposedly to look after George, but was soon taken up with MRA (Moral Re Armament) affairs. The other wives were very helpful and kind. In one sense the bottom had dropped out of his life, but at that time he was working hard, and actually it happened just before going into practice camp, - a tough period of training. He opted to stay. He could have gone back to England on compassionate grounds, but decided to stay and see it through because if he went a replacement would not be available and he knew the importance of it to the battery. On March 3rd 1937 he, Gillian, and Violet left Bangalore for England after 3 years in India.

His Battery Commander came home at the same time and he had a daughter, who looked after Gillian quite a bit on the boat. It was a three week passage through the Suez Canal. On the way out to India passengers purchased their Topi (sun proof hat) and on the way back they threw it away at Suez.

Barbara's grave at the Christian Cemetery, Bangalore. The bird bath was the original, the cross and flat stone was placed there in 2008 by Richard Grimshaw

The ships from the East always called at Plymouth and offloaded the mail that then went by train to London, it was quicker because the boat took another 3 or 4 days. They got off the boat at Plymouth and Barbara's father and mother met them and saw Gillian for the first time, and it was all rather fraught and distressing. On leave they went off on various trips. Marney, a friend, looked after Gillian, and they went down to the sea, Manorbier, Wales, on holiday. Violet was with them. There they met another poor little half orphan, a little boy whose father had died. He and his mother were there and they paired off and she went off with Violet. Then they went on another trip to a religious house parties in France and one in Angelsy. By then it was time to getting back to work - not to India of course - his time was finished there. He could have gone back to India if he had wanted, but he had been there 6 years and so he took a junior posting in England at Lichfield.

During his time on leave he spent much of his time at Levyls Dene and saw a lot of Barbara's sister Nancy. George announced his engagement to Nancy Gilliat on November 5th, and

Nancy Gilliat marries George Grimshaw at St Martha's on November 30 1937

they were married in the same month at the little chapel of St. Martha's on the Pilgrims Way on November 30th 1937, just south of Guildford and visible from Garth. Both families were very fond of it. The Gilliat family usually worshipped at the St. John's Parish Church in Merrow, but it did not seem appropriate to have the service where George and Barbara had been married only a few years before. It was a very happy outcome because it would have been very hard on Granny Gilliat if he had married outside the family, and taken Gillian away from the family.

Nancy – Her early life

Nancy was the fourth child of Algernon and Marjorie Gilliat and was born on April 6th 1914. Here follows in her own words her early life.

"I think one of my earliest recollections was when I threw a beloved little black toy dog on to the fire. I can't think why? And another time when an unloved temporary nanny laid me across her lap to dry me after my bath, and felt the indignity of it greatly. I have a violet decorated cup and saucer and plate, and remember at the age of five going into see my new baby brother Christopher (we had no idea that he was even on the way!), and being more interested in the thin bread and butter on that plate than the baby!

About the temporary nanny, she only appeared when our real Nanny took a holiday. My mother, wonderful though she was, had never bathed any of us, and had only that experience with her granddaughter Gillian.

Levyls Dene was our beautiful home for all of us. My parents lived there for 45 years, and I was born and married from there. The house stands today, but quite small. Only the C17th part remains, with all the Victorian additions demolished. There were 11 bedrooms, and a beautiful upstairs drawing room with a painting of Europa and the Bull on the ceiling. There was a painting too on the

Fourteen year old Nancy Gilliat 1928

inner drawing room ceiling. Both rooms were dark paneled with dark brown woodwork. The rooms were full of shadows and rather fearsome pictures. We would never practice the piano with the door shut. There was an old chair in the Tiger Corner that stands in our home in Devon and we always call it Tiger. There was a lovely carved staircase twisting up to the nursery at the top of the house. The night nursery and big cold bathroom, and the bachelors bedroom completed the top floor. The little Red room which later became my room was also in the vicinity of the nursery.

Nanny slept in the night nursery with the two youngest. She had wonderful auburn hair that she wore in several plats arranged around her head. It was so thick, she only washed it once a year in water.

How often one was ill in that room. About three weeks a year you reckoned to be ill with flu or some infectious disease, followed by horrible medicines and tonics. One "gargle" was so foul you had to take it in orange juice. Every Saturday mother dosed us with "Syrup of Figs", how we hated it.

After life in the night nursery I went to sleep in my parents big, cold north facing room with never a ray of sun. I remember finding my father's face very bristly when he kissed me good morning. This was a frightening room, full of dark shadows and pictures. I used to cry out for a drink to get a grown up, and I wished I had not listened to Douggie's (eldest brother) ghost stories during the day time.

It was wonderful at 8 years to move into the Little Red room behind the nursery. I loved collecting pictures and ornaments for it. I had a tiny cabinet full of little treasures I bought with my pocket money. The little window looked over the fields, thick with cowslips in the Spring. Now the fields are no more, just a big housing estate with just big trees showing that it had once been fields.

The Garden. When not out on boring walks along the Clandon Road or the Guildford Road the garden was our delight.

Bar (elder sister Barbara, George's first wife) and I were given a small garden each at the top of the orchard. I was five when I got mine – a round patch that I filled with pansies and marguerites (moon daisy). I grew a lavender bush, and Bar a white lilac. We had two grass tennis courts and had wonderful tournaments as we grew older. Mother was a very good player with her wicked underarm service. A two handed backhand and a formidable drive. She taught my brothers to play very well.

Then there was the copper beach tree and an array of hammock, seesaw, swing and trapeze. The garden was surrounded by 30 acres of fields leading onto Merrow Down. Just behind the long border, with the pink cherry blossom in spring, Bar and I even had our hidey hole where we kept all sorts of things. Jean (youngest sister) had hers in the shrubbery. There was also a top border and artichoke plants among which we would hide; and a big asparagus bed.

There was a small stone hut – in one half Pat (elder brother) kept his jars of caterpillars – the other half was an earth closet – loo. The men of the household were meant to use it, and my father handed a guest an umbrella on a wet day to go up the long path to the loo after breakfast! I can't imagine what they must have thought. There was a huge vegetable and soft fruit garden, apple orchard and potting shed where William the gardener kept his tools. There was a wonderful old yew tree in the back garden where we spent hours, and each of us had our own part of the tree. Lots of branches for acrobats and nooks for reading. If you climbed to the top you could see grown ups playing tennis – even such goddesses as the headmistress and gym mistress at the high school!

The stables and later the garages are now a lovely house. In those days the loft was a repository for many treasures – glass, china etc. as well as for apples.

My Father. When he died at 84 (hit by a car on his twice weekly walk to Guildford to buy the fish – he loved a nice Dover sole) my mother's first thought was "Blessed are the pure in heart for they shall see God". He was just that – a really good man – nothing spectacular about him, rather shy and very good tempered. We never got to know him nor felt the necessity to do so. He was our rock like lovable background. Mother really brought us up, she was the center of our lives. I don't think he minded, we relied totally on her for running the home and family..

The never quarreled. Only once did I hear him cal her "a silly little fool" when she tried to stop him going to London.

London, the City, was his other love and world and the Merchant Taylor Company his pride and joy till the war came and the wonderful old building was burned down. (He had a walking stick made from the fallen wood). He was called "The Thruster" by his friends. From the way he pushed his way through the station crowds en route to the office. He had an enormous sneeze and it was said to have knocked over a row of books on the station bookstore!

He was utterly punctual and we all knew he set the grandfather clock in the hall 5 minutes early at 7:55 am so that we would all be down for the family prayers and be ready for him to start to the station by 8:40 am. At the family prayers we all sat around on the sofa etc, and the maids filed in to sit on the dining room chairs by the windows. The cook did not come as she was preparing the huge delicious breakfast. Daddy gave us few lectures or advice, but what he said we remembered. "Never say things against your family in public," "Never discuss money," "Never lend money as it engenders ill-feeling." When something really amused him he would laugh till the tears ran down his face. He read a lot, but never imparted his knowledge to us or discussed things. He was brought up in a motherless home with his father and two brothers, and he did not marry until he was 38, eighteen years older than mother. He was immensely kind and generous to many people. Underwood, our diminutive chauffeur, spoke of him as "a real gentlemen."

My Mother. Early recognitions are wholly delightful, and I connect with her all that was happy and beautiful in those early years. As she had no chores to do for us, she was free to give herself to us on the occasions we were with her. We had a wonderful hour with her after tea in the drawing room or garden. She used to read aloud a lot, even later when we were growing up.

She always came to hear our prayers and would sing songs and hymns to us. I thought her voice was lovely till Bar told me it was very "harsh". When she was going out to dinner she would appear in an evening dress looking lovely. Her hair was golden in the early years. When old enough we came down to Sunday lunch which was a great treat. In Summer, this was followed with a walk with her on the Downs where we sat on a seat on the top ridge and she told us stories -- "Mrs.. Ponsoby" was a fat lady who did everything on the cheap, or the "Black Potato". For a great treat we went into Clanden Park to feed the swans. Then of course on Sunday we all went to church at Merrow sitting In the family pew just behind the choir.

Mother taught us lessons at five and six years old—"Reading Without Tears" and "Pot Hooks and Hangers". She taught us very well before passing us on to Durante, the governess. In spite of no chores in home and garden, mother was always busy with voluntary work. She had a "district" in Down Road. She used to visit a whole side of the street and leave Christmas presents. She also helped in the Babies Welfare, and was a keen and faithful member of the Mothers' Union. She also collected for the Waifs and Strays Society. Added to these were social function and a lot of summer tennis. We loved her reading aloud and would listen for hours.
She had her six babies in her mother's house in London or at Levyls Dene with a monthly nurse. After delivery she stayed in bed for a month and breast fed all except me as she had phlebitis and went to the south of France to recover. She had very clear and unusual writing so we had no difficulty in reading her letters.

Our lives in the first World War were not much affected and there were no relations killed. I remember Armistice Day in

Bath when I was four and the tremendous excitement.

There will be so many more vignettes of my mother. I feel that this writing is inadequate to describe her.

Nanny stayed 16 years and left when I was 13—Just as I was off to Wycombe Abbey girls school, and Chris was 8 just off to prep school. She really stayed too long to be good for us. At the age of 11, I was still having nursery tea and was very cheeky.

I never learnt to tie a tie or make my bed and was brought up to be quite impracticable. I remember being so naughty that she put her apron over her head and cried and said that she would leave, but then there was a thunder storm that night and she comforted me and did not hand in her notice. Sometimes we were sent to the night nursery as a punishment and did not return till we had said sorry, and receiving a sharp smack as she directed us back to the nursery. She was very ignorant of anything beyond our physical needs. When we asked a question she would say "Don't ask," so perhaps we stopped asking. She was deeply superstitious. It was always "They say about all sorts of subjects". Then "Who are they Nanny?" we would ask.

But how wonderful she was in illness and nursing us through all our childish complaints. And how hard she worked. Every evening when we were in bed she would sit in the backless stool and make the dresses all by herself. For a while she had a troop of nursery maids for the more menial tasks, Kate and Helen Gladwell, May Phillips, May Crust, and others. They would bring the meals from the kitchen up to the nursery. There was a running warfare between the nursery and the kitchen with the cook sending up meals via the nursery maids and returning them. In spite of all these negative memories, I think we loved her and she knew she was part of our secure little lives. Eventually she married her brother-in-law and went to live near Winchester. She saw me last when Richard was born (1938) and wanted to bathe him.

Illness and Medicine. Before the age of antibiotics I suppose we were frequently ill, either with an infectious disease (there were no inoculations in those days) or dreaded winter colds and coughs, and we were sometimes unwell for two or three weeks. After an illness we were fortified with a series of tonics, cod liver oil, malt virol (a malt extract) and Parrish's Food (a tonic made of iron sulphate and syrup). The latter was the only one we liked. Gargle was so foul it had to be drank in orange juice. Temperatures were taken very seriously, and not until 48 hours after normal could one get up from bed, so it made the illness even longer.

Old Dr. Gabb and his son Young Dr. Gabb attended us. No stethoscope for old Dr. G. just his cold ear on our chest. He was an excellent GP and knew the family well. When Mother complained of feeling rotten he merely said *"You look very well!"* When we were not ill we were dosed regularly. As a throw back to Victorian practices Mother gave us syrup of figs every Saturday night whether or not we needed it. We were also given senna pods soaked in water for the same reason.

One sometimes had neuralgia or a sick headache or felt livery with black spots dancing before ones eyes and feeling cold. I suspect we ate too much and the wrong diet

Fruit every day was not common. Later on there was a song "Eat more Fruit" so perhaps we were conscious of the need. I hated bananas, and had to sit alone on the table a whole afternoon before swallowing it.

I was very ill with whooping cough when I was six and was in bed for six weeks. I remember the lovely nursery fire on those occasions on all night. We were all ill at that time and nannie and mother looked after us. I was very weak when I got up.

The doctor always told us to put our tongues out. It seemed an important guide to the state of ones insides. Of course after breakfast each day we "did our duty" , to pee was to "make oneself comfortable". Nowadays there seem no rules at all on set times which I think is a pity, and I attribute my good health partly to these instilled habits. At Levyls Dene the ladies' loo was half way up the stairs, quite a long walk in the middle of the night. The men's loo was directly below and across from the dining room and was not considered very hygienic, and always smelled of stale cigarette smoke, so often the men had to walk up the garden path to the little house where the was a bucket loo. I can't think what men visitors must have thought when they were firmly given an umbrella and told to go up the garden path. They must have thought that we were a crazy family!

The Maids Up until the 1930s we always had four maids—cook, kitchen maid, house maid, and parlor maid. The first ones I remember were Boswell and Letts, or Lettie was we called her. We were always Miss Barbara or Miss Nancy. Only Nanny dropped the miss. Boswell and Letts were with us during the first world war. She called me her little fairy. I saw her when she was 90, still the same, sharp, humorous little person. There were an unending procession of maids and they lived in the servants' hall past the kitchen scullery and larder. We only went in that room twice a year, on Christmas Day and on our birthdays to bring some cake. We never went up the wooden staircase to their bedrooms where they went to bed by candlelight. They would use the bathroom on Sundays when we were at church. On Christmas and Easter Day they went to 6 am Communion in order to get back to do our lunch. It all sounds barbaric, but it was the way in those days and by in large they seemed happy.

The parlor maid - Annie Bird - had her own pantry where she washed up the silver and glass, cleaned the silver trimmed the oil lamps, and did the flowers. We never thought of fraternizing with the young fourteen year old kitchen maid struggling with all the plates and dishes and pots and pans. The cook was meant to be training her to become a cook eventually and of course preparing all the vegetables.

Outside there was Underwood - Undie, the chauffeur, a tiny little man who stayed for years. He had a very refined wife, Lucy. We had to see her on going and coming back from boarding school. There was William the gardener with his cracked hands and potting shed with rat's tails and horseshoes hung up, or a jay's feather. His assistant was his mentally handicapped brother, Horace, who lived with William and Mrs. Cooper. Horace was wonderful at sweeping the leaves, sharpening the knives, and cleaning all our shoes. He also managed the coal for the many fires in the house. there was no central heating. It was a huge garden for them to look after and they did it very well.

Holidays. We had two holidays in the year up until I was ten, when my grandfather died. He lived in a big Victorian house in Stoke Poges near Slough. We often went there at Easter or in June. A rather awe inspiring house with a big entrance hall and smoking room off it, and a long corridor leading to the billiard room. A stuffed tiger greeted us along that corridor and in the billiard room lived a crocodile and a cushion that played a tune when you sat on it. Of course Nanny and the nursery maid saw to it that the nursery routine went on. The nursery was dark and gloomy and our grandpa would sometimes come in to steal sugar lumps. He loved sugar and he would make his teaspoon stand up in the tea and sugar. I remember the big night nursery where the sunlight made beautiful colors on our glass ornaments. We would sometimes visit Grandpapa in the huge conservatory where he had tea among the hothouse plants. Our first sight of him was in the morning for family prayers in the dining room, attended by the whole family and the maids. The prayers were very long especially when you heard the delicious breakfast sizzling on the sideboard. Grandpapa was an ardent evangelical. He used to give us red New Testaments with the gospel versus underlined in red. He would pray aloud in his bedroom. He built St. Paul's church in Slough and founded an orphanage. The orphans would come for a day as a treat. We were snobbish and only Jean joined in the fun.

The garden was big, with smooth lawns and rhododendrons and was fun for hide-and-seek. A wall with a door led into the vegetable and fruit garden and the house farm produced butter and rich warm creamy milk for junkets.

Mr. and Mrs. Constable were Butler and Cook, and fat old Ethel loved wailing on the violin. Mrs. Constable was round and homely. Mr. Constable was more formidable with his jutting out lower lip, "Will you take a little more miss?" as he whipped our plate away!

When we were there for Easter the great excitement was to make an expedition into Slough and buy our parents horribly cheap Easter eggs. On Sundays we attended the beautiful Stoke Poges church where Grey wrote his elegy. We were fascinated by a stained glass window of a little girl and her mother floating up to heaven. We were equally fascinated by the mournful Canon Barnet who sounded as though he was about to cry. Grandpapa is buried in the churchyard.

The other visit was to the seaside in August. The big trunk was packed and we waited a good hour at the station fortified by loved comics – Rainbow and Tiger Tim and their gentle adventures. We went to Bexhill in Sussex in the early years with lodgings on the Parade, as it was easier for pram pushing. Our first treat was to go to a shop and buy small bouncing balls. We loved the rough lodgings (now promoted to private hotels and guest houses). Sand everywhere, ill fitting windows and bedrooms. The children's play room, where we ate the simple meals cooked by the landlady. Our parents had the other sitting room with the horse hair sofa for Daddy. He generally only stayed for a few days, as it was purgatory for him. He wore a very big striped bathing dress and did a header into the sea before scrambling out in a hurry. . We just lived for bathing in those early years. You paddled for the first few days, to get used to it, and wore voluminous paddlers. To keep dry when it was cold. Nanny would be on the beach with a big towel. We would then run up and down the beach to warm up, and Mother would arrive with lots of shiny 1/2d buns. – a great treat. Mother had to do all the shopping for the landlady. The meals were very simple. Boiled fowl, runner beans, and plums and custard. We always had to wait for two hours after meals before bathing, and then there was wonderful reading aloud from Mother.

After the summer holiday we arrived home to find the maids, gardener and chauffeur had spring cleaned the house and beaten the carpets on the back lawn - all this before the days of vacuum cleaners and fitted carpets, or washing machines. What a sheltered and privileged life we led.

Christmas I am nearly 77 and those Christmas days are still so vivid and close. It started a few days before when we all went to Mother's shop on the dinning room table. As our pocket money was so meager – 1d, 2d and 3d per week – Mother devised a good way of helping us to shop. She laid in lots of little things that made it possible for us to shop within our means with none of the exhaustion for Mother taking us into Guildford. I remember on our dull walks on the appropriate day we would recite "the day after tomorrow we will be able to say, the day after tomorrow will be Christmas Day".

The Christmas tree went up to the ceiling and there were very big toys. Sometimes there was a conjurer and a talking doll. I was always overawed by the grown ups hovering around. The seemed like goddesses and there was none of the familiarity you have today. The games Oranges and Lemons and Hunt the Thimble used to fill a shy child with embarrassment!

We never did any decorating ourselves, and to have brought holly into the house before the day was considered unlucky. We were awake early on Christmas morning poking with our toes against the net stockings, and then all the squeals of excitement. We loved the firework sparklers. After we were confirmed the stocking rather faded out. Because we were off to church at 8.00 am., though I remember one year we had them in the afternoon. We lay on the nursery floor in the dark and stockings were delivered. After another service at 11am we went home for the usual wonderful lunch. I hated Christmas pudding, but kind Aunt Nell used to give me her 3d bit.. I loved collecting pictures off the crackers for my scrapbook.

All afternoon we spent in opening our presents, all in brown paper and arranged on separate tables. My special treasures were a wax baby doll and a wooden farm which sad to say got lost, and anyway I was only allowed to play with them on Sundays.

Christmas tea followed (how we had room for it I don't know). One year we found tiny decorated trees on our plates. One of the children took slices of cakes to the servants hall. We only went there twice a year with the slices of cakes – Christmas and birthdays.

One year Pat recited the hymn "A few more years should roll" – rather depressing for Christmas. We played paper and pencil games in the evening and perhaps charades. Then there was supper and depending on our ages BED.

The Christmas holidays were always full of parties. We wore white frilly dresses over frilly pants, bronze stockings and shoes. One year we wore rose pink velvet dresses all alike, and passed them down. So Jean must have been tired of the velvet dress after Bar and I passed them to her. Parties were wonderful.

Our party games included Oranges and Lemons, Blinds Man Buff, General Post, Jacob and Rachel, and Dumb Crambo. Charades was very popular. My mother was brilliant at her Punch and Judy show. Later she performed them for her grandchildren adding topical features to the traditional show. She enjoyed life so much herself and was always such an enthusiast. After she died someone said she was a "life enhancer".

As we lived on Merrow Downs, there was wonderful tobogganing just outside our fields and people came from far and wide to spin down the slopes.

Education. There were no play groups or nursery schools in those days. Mother taught us at the age of five to read from the Victorian book "Reading without Tears" and writing by "Pot Hooks and Hangers". Durante, our Governess, took over when we were six. She came daily on her bicycle from Guildford, having first been to Communion at St. Nicholas'.

She had no training but was a natural teacher. She taught Pat, Douggie and Bar till they were eight and nine and ready for school. She had a great love for nature study. I remember how we found a lark's nest in the grass on the Downs. We learnt to paint by brushwork flowers and berries.

At the age of seven I went to Guildford to share a governess with about six other children. "Auntie" Ra at Sheaves House taught us very well. I wrote a long story at seven years eight months that was typed out as a book, but alas was lost! I thought I would be an author when I grew up. I used to write books for Mother for her birthday. Alas as years went by my imagination became stultified, though I was always good at English. When I was twelve I wrote a play for me and my friends to perform. Mother invited her friends to watch and we made £5 to help a little girl in the slums called Daisy. We used to rehearse in the playground in the break at the High School. Our village school in Merrow was for children up to the age of 14. After that a few were bright enough to go to the Grammar and County schools. Over the door was a sign "The fear of the Lord is the beginning of wisdom."

I will always remember the devoted spinster teachers at the High School: Martha Nye – Math, and Miss Peel – History. We learnt a lot of poetry including "Hiawatha" and we acted the Red Piper with me being the Piper.

The science labs were pathetic, and a far cry from those of today. What horrible lunches we ate in the hall. I had to swallow lumps of fat whole rather than leave them. The water tasted horrid, but we all survived.

The High School was a church school and we were well taught in religion. Though I can't remember anything specific. We always had a holiday on Ascension Day. There were many girls from the local shops, but we were not allowed to invite them home as they were in the "trade", not even the distinguished looking Francis family who were in "coal". What snobbery! There was one Roman Catholic girl, Winnie Bracken, and we were always asking her about "Confession". School fees were £7 per term in those days. Playground games were Hopscotch, String Hi, and Touch Last. We often fell on the concrete playground making huge holes in our black woolen stockings.

Books Before the age of radio and TV books were our solace. We had a long row of nursery books and read them over and over again, generally lying on our tummies.

We read all Mrs. Molesworth's (1839-1921) books: "Peep behind the Sashes" and "Froggy and Bunny", and earlier ones as well from our Grannies collection. "Sweet Content" was a much loved. The modern book of that day was "Knock Three Times" – much loved by us. Our children and now our grandchildren liked it. It was falling apart, so a kind niece had it mended and it is as good as ever. Later on there were the school girl books Angela Brazil (1867-1947) and lovely Christmas annuals and "Little Folk" magazines. We did read more advanced books, "Jane Eyre" being my first grown up book.

My Mother used to read aloud to us and we loved it. It went on until I was grown up expecting Richard! At one time she used to read exciting anti Roman catholic books which she got from Robin's grandmother at a time when RCs were regarded as "of the devil". I have still got Lilian Golden's "Houses" – given me by Kit Taylor written around 1860.

Daddy got us "Children's Newspaper" to read, but we found it excessively boring with no gossip or juicy bits – all very "improving". I can't think who read it. Of course Mother read us "Pilgrims Progress" which was fascinating and in our edition had wonderful pictures. How rarely do modern children know anything about it.

Religion. The whole of my life has been shot through with religion, and at the end of it I feel that I have hardly begun.
We were taught to say our prayers every night at our mother's knee. "God bless Mummy and Daddy, brothers, sisters, aunties, uncles, cousins and all kind friends". Oh yes we remembered Grandpa, but Granny's name was de-linked after she

died. You did not pray for the dead!

Mother faithfully taught us all she knew, and read us books like "Peep of Day" and "Line upon Line", the standard religious books for children. She always sang us hymns at night, which I loved including "Ninety and Nine" and "Sun of my Soul". We attended church from a very early age. Before Bar could read she opened her mouth and pretended to sing in case the clergyman got angry with her.

We always went to Matins and sat behind the choir in Merrow church. We had our own pew, and Daddy had his big black prayer book. There were familiar faces in the choir like William the gardener and Mr. Day the boot-maker. Everybody turned to the East during the Creed except us. Daddy was very low Church. We used to feel like early Christian martyrs standing up for the "Right". As I grew older I compromised with a semi-turn! I can see all the people in the pews behind us. Aunt Nell, Miss Ashby, Mrs.. Power and Mrs. Carlton. Nearly everyone attended church in those days - the gentry in the morning, and the village people in the evening. The women would have cooked the Sunday dinner. We were privileged to have a cook to do ours!

Sunday afternoon was always a treat as Mother took us for a walk up the valley on the ridge and told us stories – "The Black Potato" and Mrs.. Ponsoby". I am sure that the seats we sat on along the ridge have disappeared long ago. After tea on Sundays we would sing hymns in the drawing room, each choosing their favourite. We hated Daddy's choice!

In the early Spring time when we likened to "Little Blossoms rare" Chris used to love the tea total hymn "Have Courage my Boy to say No", only he always sang "have Cu Cu my boy" as he couldn't talk plainly until he was five.

I have forgotten to mention the daily family prayers when Daddy sat at the dining room table and read from a huge family Bible. We sat on sofas and chairs, and I used to be fascinated by the pools of green light made by pressing ones fingers in the eye while buried on the sofa on my knees. The maids used to file in and sit on chairs. The cook didn't come in because she was cooking a delicious breakfast. What enormous meals they were. 2 eggs for the men and a delicious fish or sausage dish sizzling on a silver dish., with methylated spirits keeping it hot from underneath.

I sometimes wonder how we would have developed as a family if we had not met with Mrs. "Lanky", Robin Lankester's mother, and the new world that she opened. She and Dr.. "Lanky" had just arrived from India, where they had been missionaries, and he was now a doctor in Guildford.

Mother at the age of 40 was converted in the evangelical sense and life became new. She began to read and study the Bible, and go to conventions and meetings. She made new friends in the "Officers Christian Union". She gave up bridge parties and such like worldly pursuits, but she continued to take the family to Switzerland after Christmas and thus avoided the dance invitations which were considered worldly. Tennis was a great outlet and we had wonderful tennis parties. Mother was very good and taught Douggie and Pat to play so well.

We came into it all when I was 8 and it made an impression on me. I loved Mother so much, I felt that it must be true is she believed it. I remember asking her about the Cross when I was 11. Yet I could never feel converted and never have to this day.

I think with Mother it was a new stage in her pilgrimage as religion had always meant a lot to her, but now had found fulfillment. I think I have read the Bible almost everyday since I was seven when Bar and I joined the Scripture Union at Bexhill CSSM. I don't think that Douggie was very interested and managed to steer clear. Pat was converted at Bude CSSM when he was 14 and never looked back.

I suppose a lot of it was second hand, we never questioned or discussed. If we criticised a sermon Mother didn't like it. She said "It may have helped someone". We grew up feeling different from the local young people which was not really good. Religion combined with a very tender conscience and worrying nature made school days very difficult.

Wycombe Abbey It was really a shock to suddenly go to boarding school after a very sheltered existence at home and Nanny had only just left when Chris was eight and I was thirteen. I was following in the steps of Bar who was so clever, talented and good at work and games. I just scraped into the school in the bottom form, but moved up the following term. I was very homesick and whenever I ran into Bar, I wept! I was youngest in the dormitory – "Big Red Left " and had to take down the monitors laundry etc.

There were about 30 in the House "Rubens" and house order was very important to us, and you went up and down according to your behaviour. You stood in a circle after lunch in House Order when 'the Gem' came in and we had to say what we would be doing that afternoon. I far too often had to say "may I be kept in please?" for forgetting to hand in my prep. I would then have to explain and have another a row with the Gem after House Order.

We played lacrosse and cricket in the afternoon – I was hopeless at both and also gym. I always dreaded the latter, and envied the girls with the "curse" who sat and watched! Mother came to see us three times a term. We were never allowed home, and there was no half term. Bliss when she took us out to lunch in Wycombe or Beaconsfield.

I remember crying all through lunch just after three friends had chucked me, I felt it was the end of the world. I remember Sally Sprock turning against me saying "I was pink and white and pi religious". It was devastating. I learnt elocution and loved it. One year in the competition Bar won the Senior Prize and I the Junior. Maybe my only success.

Every Sunday we went for walks "Heads and Tails". The two heads were "oldies" and the tails had to follow at a reasonable distance where the others led! In the summer term we had "sit outs' in the grounds instead of walks. You arranged the walks and who you were going with at the start of each term. You chose your best friend for first and last walks. What an extraordinary custom, and so different from today. You had to have a best friend for going to chapel, lectures and concerts. Eventually after being "chucked" I palled up with Bessie Breargood. I didn't especially like her, but she was on her own, so it was convenient.

At the start of each term we had "bug hunting' or hair brushing to make sure that we had picked up nothing on the train. Also temperatures were taken morning and evening as there were always infectious illnesses about. I never had a day in the hospice until my last term when the school went down with flu and nurses were sent down from Westminster Hospital in London to nurse us.. Even though my temperature never exceeded 99°F we were not allowed out of bed for a week.

No man ever entered our lives except the innocuous Mr. Float, the rector who talked about "Heaven or that other place", and Stanley Merchant, organist of St. Paul's, who came once a week for singing. I remember with delight "The Lady of Shallot" and "Revenge". We had concerts by famous people like Solomon Myrna, and Jolly D"Aram. We had to attend in our white dresses. All lost on me sad to say! We also attended lantern lectures that were really interesting. Miss Grostwaite "auntie" always replied thanking for a fascinating lecture. – laughter!

The boot-room was a dark room where we had our lockers for outdoor equipment; we also had cocoa and soup there in the morning. The house study was where we did our prep with a desk and locker and where special treasures and photos were arranged. Only in my last years did the monitors have their own small study. It is all such a long time ago – 65 years ago – when I just entered in 1927, but it seems clear as yesterday. None of our children went to Wycombe. We couldn't afford it anyway. Gillian failed the entrance exam to my distress – she had been to a hopeless small school where she wasn't coached at all. However she got on fine when we went

Page 109

to Africa and got her A levels and a degree at Bristol University.

The strange closed world of boarding school. I failed School Certificate, hearing the news on Christmas Day in a card from "Auntie". "I am so sorry you failed, the arithmetic and chemistry were not good enough". I should have been made to retake it, but I wasn't, and sailed into the Upper Vith to do English with people going to University, and fear I rather wasted my time and achieved nothing.

Bar got her Higher Certificate – not many girls achieved that. She could have gone to University or on the stage. When "Auntie" asked her what she would like to do Bar said "*get married*". I think "Auntie" was quite shocked and surprised, but that is just about what Bar did – to George.

George and Nancy – the start of a 63 year marriage

Shortly after marrying Nancy on November 30th 1937, George was posted to his new Regiment, a mobile antiaircraft regiment at Whittington Barracks near Lichfield.

They arrived in Lichfield, and wasn't very popular because he was married, so he had to find somewhere to live. The army wouldn't help because one wasn't supposed to be married in those days, they preferred one to be living in sin! His battery commander had them for a night or two then he found a very nice farm house that was a mile or two outside Lichfield. The farmer's wife was a very good cook, she produced the most marvelous souffles. That is where George and Nancy started their life. It was a bit cramped and it was quite a long way to go to feed the horses. So they didn't stay for very long, but they had a very nice time there; the farmer's wife was very helpful, she helped Nancy a lot.

It was there that Gillian had her crisis, she contracted pneumonia. She very nearly died, but she was treated with the first M&B (sulphur drug); the doctor told them that there was a real crisis and if they would agree to try this new drug he could try it to see if it has any effect. Nancy and George were at their wits end and there was nothing else to do, so they said yes. It worked fortunately, she recovered from the crisis. It was difficult for Nancy because she felt responsible (Nancy always felt some guilt whenever troubles occurred, mainly because she had little understanding of technical and science issues) it was a very cold spell and she wouldn't let Gillian get out and run and walk, she thought she would be warmer in the pram and also they got along quicker and Nancy was warm because she was pushing the pram, but Gillian was complaining that she was cold.

They found a house in Lichfield, in Whittington Court, a great big Victorian hulk of a house that they rented for £1 a week. There was some kind of heating, the rooms were enormous, It was pretty cold. Nancy was pregnant but she went down to Guildford to be with her mother for the birth (September 15th 1938). She wasn't a bit happy in Guildford, and when George went down to see so her, he got an ambulance and brought her back to Whittington Court. In the meantime he had been able to get a lot of redecoration done that was ready for her return; the weather was getting warmer.

George had two horses and used to hunt regularly in his tailcoat and top hat. There were two hunts, the South and North Staffordshire Hunts were mainly the ones he hunted with, occasionally he joined another, but that took a long time because he couldn't afford a box so he had to ride his horse there and ride back again. He used to hunt twice a week.

There was not a lot else to do. The gunners had to practice their shooting. On one occasion he got into trouble with the Sergeant Major when he first arrived there because, of course, after coming from India, where there were set procedures for looking after these critical animals one of which was after returning from parade, the first thing one did was to clean down the horses, wipe them down, water them and feed them; and until this had done no-one was allowed to leave the lines.
The first time he went out for a practice with the lorries pulling the guns, they were mechanised by then, he said to the Sgt.

Major, *"well come on, we must clean everything up before we go"* and he said *"What?"* *"Well surely we clean everything before we go don't we, we always had to clean our horses, water them and feed them, surely we should clean up the lorries and fill them up for the next trip."* *"Oh no, we don't do anything like that here"*.

He was put in his place properly by the Battery Sgt. Major. He went off to lunch and came back after lunch and sorted it out. It was traditional that the horses were cleaned up, fed, and watered before going off to do other things. The SM ought to have been impressed by that really. Perhaps he was, but he wasn't going to show it, afraid he might insist on it as common practice which it should have been. But any rate, he had a good time there. They were just practicing, that's all one could do, practice your gun drill.

Whilst in Lichfield George went to Mannabier for anti-aircraft practice for a week or two, and Nancy went too. They used to go to Mannabier on holiday before that, but it was also Practice Camp for anti-aircraft. They had digs there and they would get up and practice shooting at a moving object with live ammunition. They shot at a drogue - sort of wind sock towed by an aeroplane. The aeroplane was far enough away to be pretty sure one missed it, hopefully. He didn't recall ever hitting the drone; it was all guesswork really, one had an elementary computer in the aiming box, the latter was a great big thing on a tripod which one looked through and it had a sort of computer inside it which was supposed to help one get on target, but it was very much hit and miss. Those Practice Camps were rather good fun.

At that time he was still only a Lieutenant. He had two guns that he was responsible for. He was made Camp Adjutant, which was a rather boring job, doing all the ordinary chores. They had no excitement untill somebody tried to land an aeroplane in the middle of Camp and ran into a few of the tents and knocked them down. He went to the Regimental Commander and said, *"Look I don't think this is a very good idea, to land our aeroplanes in the middle of the camp"*. The aeroplanes used to come back after practice. He said he thought they ought to land somewhere else. The Commander said that it wouldn't happen again - it was just a one off. That was the attitude in those days. So nothing happened. Then there was a big property owner, who used to lay on lovely strawberry tea parties, that they were all invited to, which was rather good.

This was just an interlude; all of a sudden, war seemed to loom over the horizon. Life became a bit more serious. George was moved off to Biggin Hill (subsequently a very importat airfield in the Battle of Britain), in Kent, and was appointed Liaison Officer between the Army and the Air Force. They moved home, and rented a lovely house on the Pilgrim Way at Westerham for £1 a week. More or less the standard rent in those days. These houses would just be empty. In those days, they could have bought both those houses for £1200 or £1800 but they didn't have the money, nor did they think of doing it. He might have borrowed some money from his father-in-law but the latter had never bought his house, he had rented Levyls Dene for 40 years. In those days it was part of the Onslow Estate and one just rented it. They still had candles and gas lamps, even after 40 years. And of course if one live in that sort of environment one don't think of buying.

The nanny at Westerham had a room at the back of the house that looked over the garden. There were lots of rabbits and it annoyed George that she wouldn't get up in the morning, so

George and Nancy at Westerham , just before the War

he decided he would get her up. He went into her room and shot rabbits with a shotgun. It certainly got her up.

George was sent back to the Brigade and became Q Captain, and before he knew where he was he was off to France. To war.

Nancy was left at Westerham, and she had to pack up the house and everything and get herself back to Levyls Dene. He and Nancy said goodbye on Waterloo Bridge. She went to Levlys Dene where she remained with Gillian and Richard for most of the war.

War time Levyls Dene

Nancy, Gillian and Richard stayed at Levyls Dene from 1940 to 1945. It was an interesting time, although quite protected, as the Guildford area was not generally a target of the German Luftwaffe. Like all other homes the house followed a strict black out. The Gilliats maintained their household through out the war. Mrs. Cooper, the cook, controlled the kitchen, Annie Bird, the parlor maid, was a special favorite of the children. Then there was William Cooper the gardener, and his brother, Horace, who looked after the coal, sharpened the knives – and they were sharp.

Underwood (Undie) the chauffeur was another favorite. The household was well fed generally; William had a large vegetable garden and many domesticated rabbits that were bred regularly. They ate a lot of rabbit and horse meat during those war years. Underwood maintained his domain in the separate garage building with a small workshop where Richard spent much of his time.

This large house had no central heating – the house was warmed by coal and log fires and in the bedrooms by the honeycombed type gas fires. All the lighting was by gaslight. Annie used to come around in the evenings lighting the gaslights. There were no washing machines. The laundry was sent out – collected and returned by a laundry man. Plumbing was simple

– all lead pipes in those days! Imagine the health concerns – and lead paint too. There were no more than three bathrooms for this large household. The kitchen was the warmest room in the house, where there was a coal fired range presided over by the marvelous Mrs. Cooper. What delicious breakfasts – egg, bacon, sausage, smoked cod, and lots and lots of toast and piping hot coffee. Lunch was normally cold roast beef or cold mutton. The deserts were wonderful: summer pudding, trifles, rice pudding, fruit salads in the summer, ices and so on. She made the best sponge cake in the world, and at Christmas, excelled with Christmas pudding and Christmas fruit cake with marzipan and rock hard icing.

George and Nancy with Richard and Gillian in 1940 at Levlyls Dene, just prior to George's posting to East Africa

The first change that occurred at Levlys Dene was the arrival of the Women's Land Army together with their Ford tractors (steel lugged wheels) to plough up all the pastures and plant them to wheat. Then came 30 child refugees from London who lived in a large wooden hut that had been constructed outside on the driveway in front of the house.

When the London Blitz really got going underway, the air raid sirens signaling an imminent raid and the subsequent "all clear" were regular occurrences on most days during 1941. There was no air raid shelter at the house, and the best cover was considered under the main stairways. Two bombs were jettisoned by a fleeing German bomber and blew up in the nearby newly planted wheat. That was the closest call of the whole war. Later when Germany started sending flying bombs "doodlebugs" at London, on many occasions the doodlebugs would cut their engines in the Guildford area to begin the glide path to London.

Richard recalls that the only time as a young boy he saw the grownups seriously disturbed was when listening to the 6.00 pm news on May 24 1941 when they learnt that the Battle Cruiser – H.M.S. Hood had been sunk by the Bismark in the Battle of Denmark Strait with only 3 survivors out of a crew of 1421. That was indeed a somber evening. Another occasion was when the news came that Christopher Gilliat, Nancy's younger brother, who was a flight Lieutenant in the RAF Bomber Command, was killed on September 3rd 1943 on a bombing raid to Germany. He is buried at the Rheinberg War Cemetery 85 km north of Cologne.

Earlier that year on January 13th 1943 George's mother, Violet, died of cancer at the age of 57. Richard recalls Nancy going to the funeral, and while she was away he found a Singer sewing machine attachment that was very sharp, and managed to inflict a deep cut on his knee. Earlier, on April 17th 1942, George's brother Tommy died of consumption at the age of 34. He was buried in the churchyard of St Martha's on the Pilgrim's Way, not far from Garth and Gratton's in the heart of the Surrey countryside that they all loved so much. Violet was buried next to him.

There were fairly regular visits to see Granny Grimshaw (Violet) who lived with Aunt Ella (her sister) in Horseshoe Lane at the other end of Merrow; as well as occasional visits to other Aunts and Uncles. Once or twice Nancy took the children to London to buy shoes and clothes, but apart from these visits, war years were confined to Levyls Dene and it surrounds. Walks to Merrow church and a farm to see the cows. Undie built the children toboggans there always seemed to be plenty of snow in those days. Occasionally they would visit Granny Gilliat's sister, Aunt Cissie, she always had what seemed huge and complex jigsaw puzzles spread out on a special table by the window.

Petrol was strictly rationed and yet occasionally the family went for a drive chauffeured by Undie at a very stately pace.- at night the headlights were restricted to a slot of light. The other rationing was food. Each person had a buff colored ration book that allocated food and clothing. There always seemed to be enough shredded wheat cereal, milk and orange juice for the children. Granny Gilliat managed the food and lives of the family – she always did it so well. She was a special much loved Granny to all the Grandchildren, right until she died at the age of 93. She was a true matriarch and kept the family ties close.

The life of the children seemed to continue along the lines that Nancy was brought up. The top floor nursery complex was under the control of Richard's Nanny Watts for a while. He remembers visits from his cousin Peter and Margaret Gilliat (Pat's son and daughter) and later David and Tim Lankester (Jean and Robin's two sons). They played and fought hard.

Gillian and Richard visiting Granny (Violet Grimshaw) in Guildford, 1942

Gillian slept in the little room behind the nursery. There were still coal fires and gas lamps throughout the house, and morning prayers in the dining room. Granny Gilliat was a wonderful impersonator and everyone loved her very professional "Punch and Judy" shows that she normally performed in the large downstairs dining room. There were no toys to speak of during the war. The children made use of old family toys – dolls – wind up trains – and meccano. When a doll needed

A war time (1943) photo of Nancy with Gillian and Richard

mending they went to the "Dolls Hospital in Swan Lane in Guildford.

The tennis courts were still occasionally used, one was now strictly for croquet. The tennis courts had netting surrounds in which, regularly in those days, prickly hedgehogs would get caught and had to be released. The great beech tree and yew tree, so familiar to Nancy as a child, remained great attractions to Richard and Gillian and their visiting cousins and friends.

Everybody loved Levyls Dene. It had a special ambience about it, and of course, to the younger generation it provided great security. The gardens and grounds set in a valley in the Surrey Downs was a very special and "warm" and exciting place. The house was rather dark and ghostly, but it was full of care and love, and that was what was really important,
George came back on leave twice during the war - once in 1941 and again in 1944. At that time (1944) he bought back Garth and reinstalled Nancy and her children there in time for John's birth in July 1945.

Captain George Grimshaw – at War

France. At the beginning of the Second World War George was mobilized and went to Portsmouth to board a destroyer for France. Two or three destroyers were going over as the advance guard for various formations, and were to be the first landings in France. They were all staff officers going over to prepare the ground and plan and develop an operational strategy. They were the first people to go and there. On that occasion was a certain amount of alarm at Portsmouth that German submarines might enter, and they wanted to close the torpedo nets across the entrance between the forts and the main land, but George's destroyer couldn't make it because it had got a rope round its propeller, and in truly nautical fashion they were all summoned by the skipper and told to stand in the bows and jump to see if they could raise the stem enough to free it from the rope; it wasn't successful, he couldn't imagine why they thought it would be. Anyway eventually a diver had to be called, and if there is one person in the world who can't be hurried it's a diver. He took ages getting his gear on and getting underneath the boat and cutting the rope and when it was finally cut it was all stations go. It was practically dark by then.

The boat zig zagged across the English Channel to Cherbourg where they disembarked and parked for the night in a nunnery of all places. There were still nuns there. Charming nuns all going round in their veils, seeing that they had tea and hot drinks and no doubt they were a bit surprised at what they saw. People were not very careful about whether they undressed or didn't undress. By then they all wanted to go to bed and sleep. The next day they were put in coaches and sent down to Nantes where they again had great discussions with the French commander of the city as to where they would be billeted and whether they should occupy a school or not, they were there for about 48 hours. Then they moved to Lille, where they decided where the British army was to be deployed, and then they were sent up to the French border. They were all officers and office staff, the troops hadn't arrived. They were given their area where they were to be deployed and then the troops did arrive, but the weather was so appalling and the conditions so awful that the quartermaster and George felt that the best thing he could possibly do was to go and buy up all the corrugated iron or anything to make a shelter for the troops which they duly did. George was given a very nice chap, French translator, interpreter, and who took him round and they looked round all the industrial centres where they thought there might be something and they bought up all the corrugated iron they could see. He then organised lorries to go and pick it up and the troops then made themselves quite reasonably comfortable. They dug down because they might have been attacked. He didn't know how they drained their holes but still at least they had a roof over their heads. Then George went home because by then it was getting on for Christmas. He was sent to the Staff College at Camberley. Nancy joined him there and they rented yet another house.

England. Such was the phoney war, it was more or less like peace time, except they knew they only had a few months for training instead of the normal two years. This was 1940. The house they rented was a dreary row house. It was a terribly cold winter and all the pipes burst and he had to go up into the roof and stretch wrap the pipes in rubber strips to try and stop the flow, otherwise they would have been flooded out. He managed to staunch it enough to carry on. Nancy had a tough time, they were always moving around from one place to another. One of his Instructors, Col. Horrocks, became a Field Marshall. The course was just pure concentrated instruction really. They used to work out exercises without troops on the ground, but there was no parading or anything like that, it was just school. They had lectures about all sorts, tactics and logistics etc. They were there for about 3 months and it was well into Spring of 1940 when he was posted to Scotland as a staff officer of 51 Scottish Division located in Perth.

Again he was moved, this time to Southern Command. He went to Porton Gas centre just outside Salisbury. (It's quite important now) - they sent all poison gas they discovered to Porton. He was picked out as one of the top people at College to go and study gas warfare.

After that he was sent down to Ganville, which is the west side of Plymouth on the far side of Fern Head; it was an exposed miserable place too, Still he got some good fishing there. Nancy followed him around, with the children. They were just living out of their bags and suitcases really. She found digs somewhere. There were some good times. They were reforming after Dunkirk and in some places he found himself with only a skeleton staff, there with nothing much to do.

East Africa. In 1941 he was posted to East Africa because the Italians had poison gas in Abyssinia. He and a chemist, a civilian, were sent off to Nairobi, where he was billeted with some very nice people just across the road from the headquarters, to pick up any information they could as to whether the Italians had gas; and if they did, where was it, because it depended a good deal on where it was and whether it might be used as to where they should plan the invasion from the south. George's group was to invade from the south and another group the north. Following the invasion gas was found - but it was never used.

Having organised the stacking, deployment of the anti-gas equipment. One of George's jobs was to try and see whether it was a physical possibility to wear western anti-gas equipment in the tropical conditions that was expected in in Abyssinia and Somaliland. He took a party of people down to the Athi River (just south of Nairobi), which was the hottest place he could think of. He made them all get into this anti-gas equipment and it was absolutely hell. The temperature was about 100° F outside let alone inside the anti-gas gear. They were just pouring sweat and they marched together up the river bank, to test the equipment. Before long the unit doctor said that he thought they had all had enough. Anyway that was the only time he led a gas attack! They knew it was possible and that that was an extreme case, but up in the cooler highlands of Abyssinia it would be reasonable. Another thing he had to work out was the packing of the equipment for a whole battalion. 600 to 800 sets of anti-gas equipment takes a bit of loading into one one vehicle.

A war time picnic in Kenya. Circa 1941

He then ceased to concentrate on gas and was promoted to Colonel and was AfC 1 Ops and was left behind to run the show in Nairobi when the troops all moved up north. Once the battle line had been started he was out of it, and after that he was responsible for training Kenyans. The nearest occasion to real war he got was when he had to walk between two lines of machine guns firing at him. That was part of the training.

The Ally troops were advancing rapidly from Mogadishu (Italian Somaliland) and other places up the coast. The Italians ran away so quickly - one only had to get behind the Italians and they would generally quickly retreat, so they spent the whole time trying to get behind them. They were running out of local guards for Mogadishu and other places.

On one occasion when he managed to rustle up a whole battalion of African troops, equip them and get them on a train down to Mombasa in 24 hours. That was quite an achievement really, bringing them from about 80 miles away, to Nairobi Railway Station, where they were equipped with the proper clothing, rifles etc. and putting them on a train to Mombasa, onto a ship, all within about 24 hours. He recalls all of them sitting round the table at Headquarters in Nairobi, every branch of the staff - each one had his job to do, it was all done in 24 hours. George was the coordinator, it wasn't difficult, he only told them what to do and they went off and did it.

Abyssinia. He went eventually to Abyssinia to see what was going on. A background to the Abyssinia campaign follows.

Abyssinia was occupied by Mussolini and his Italian army through a series of battles between October 1935 and May 1936, because it was one of the few places in Africa that had not been colonized and had great natural resources. (736,000 died in those 6 months).

The World War II Abyssinia campaign was a direct consequence of Mussolini's declaration of war on Britain and France on 10 June 1940. The British, fearing that the enemy in Libya and Italian East Africa might jointly threaten Britain's position in Egypt, Sudan, and the Middle East, and realizing the potential military value of the Ethiopian 'Patriots', who had never surrendered to the invaders, flew Emperor Haile Selassie from Britain to Sudan in July. They later despatched two British officers, Brig. Dan Sandford and Col. Orde Wingate into Gojjam to make contact with the Patriots, in August and November respectively. Meanwhile the Italians overran British Somaliland in August. The Allied campaign against Italian East Africa opened on 19 January 1941, when British and Indian forces under Gen Sir William Platt (George's commanding general) advanced from Sudan into Italian Eritrea. On the following day, and almost 200 miles (320 km) to the south, the emperor, with Wingate as his principal adviser, entered Gojjam, also from Sudan. Four days later, and almost 1,000 miles (1,600 km) to the south-east, British, East African, and South African forces under Gen Sir Alan Cunningham struck from Kenya into Italian Somalia. The Italian forces, which had been isolated from metropolitan Italy for half a year and were demoralized by four years of Ethiopian Patriot activity, put up weaker resistance than initially anticipated. British Commonwealth forces from the south captured Mogadishu, capital of Somalia, on 25 February, and swept northwards to Jigjiga, on 17 March, and Harar, ten days later. Allied forces from the west meanwhile captured Keren, after fierce fighting, on 26 March, and Asmara, capital of Eritrea, on 1 April. The emperor's army, though poorly armed and often lacking air support captured Debra Marqos, capital of Gojjam, on 10 April. The Patriots under Ras Abeba Aregai meanwhile consolidated themselves around Addis Ababa. The capital itself fell shortly afterwards, on 6 April, to South African troops. The emperor returned on 5 May, exactly five years after its capture by Gen Badoglio. The next few months were spent in 'mopping up'. This ended with the fall of Gondar to the British and the Patriots on 27 November. Ethiopia thus became the first country to be freed from Axis conquest.

By the time George got there the Italians had been driven out of Somaliland. He drove his car from Mogadishu up to British Somaliland, and through British Somaliland to Abyssinia via Hargeisa. Whilst driving across the desert he drove through a swarm of locusts, which was quite an experience, because they were absolutely thick, and he had to slow down to almost walking pace as the locusts were just sweeping in a great cloud across the road - they were probably more dangerous than the Italians!

The army had moved on and he linked up with General Platt, who was his boss, and briefed him as to what was going on back at base. He met with Platt and his Chief of Staff, who was a tall ex-guardsman at Jigjiga. They were on Jijiga Airfield, recently recaptured, and were just standing there talking when they suddenly realised there was an Italian aircraft coming out of the sky from nowhere and there seemed to be a lot of bullets flying around the place; his instinct was to take cover instantly, but the guardsman was not going to be made to run for anything, he stood up straight and walked very slowly towards some shelter. By that time the aircraft had gone and fortunately hadn't hit any of them. But it was the sort of instinctive difference between himself, ready to plunge into any cover, and the guardsman who was going to stand upright and face the enemy. Of course Jijiga was the site where, Col. Wilson, who got a V.C. for the gallant way he fought off the Italian machine gun post and was supposed to have been killed. He received a posthumous V.C. but after the War he suddenly turned up, and the story goes that he was told that he'd got a posthumous V.C. which had been presented to his mother, so he went off to his mother and said *'hi, I want my V.C.'* and she said *'not a bit of it, it was given to me, it's mine'*!

From Jigjiga George continued to Addis Ababa itself. Addis

Ababa is the capital of Ethiopia, Abyssinia as it used to be; one drove down the escarpment, across the bottom of Great Rift Valley and up again on the other side. The Italians were nearly at the end of their tether, but on the way up he visited Harar, which was the capital of one of the provinces and down in the valley there was a Coptic church and so he naturally went on the church, and he received a very warm welcome from the priest, who took him around and eventually showed him the tabernacle which was the great centre of the church. He was very friendly because the Italians just fired their guns and left holes in the wall.

He stayed a couple of days in Addis Ababa and then flew back in a captured German plane that was made of "corrugated iron", the wings flapped violently.

Kenya. Back in Kenya a lot of Italian prisoners were arriving and they had to be put to work. They were used to build a new road down the Rift Valley escarpment (Nairobi – Naivasha) because the Italians were very good at road making. Eventually there was a very nice road. It went from Nairobi to the escarpment and then down the escarpment, which was very steep to the floor of the Great Rift Valley. They also built a very pretty chapel near the bottom of the escarpment road. Initially it was a beaten earth road, then it became eventually tarmac. Most of the time George had a driver. He was always was allotted a driver, It was a perfectly ordinary type of civilian car painted khaki that was all, Vauxhall or an American Chevrolet or a Jeep.

Nancy never joined George in East Africa. He was living with some very nice people opposite his headquarters in Muthaiga. His host was the Secretary of the East Africa Mining & Power Company (Kit Taylor's husband – a Ringmore friend - was the Chairman). They were a very nice couple and had two young boys.

Fairly soon after the Abyssinian campaign was over the military planners had to rethink what was going to happen to all the African troops and how they were going to be organised and deployed. It was decided that there should be two African divisions, an East African Division and a West African Division. General Platt, who was George's commanding General, went back to England to develop a strategy as to what should be done. Platt took George along as his staff officer. They flew back in one of the Empire Flying Boats following the River Nile. He was always terribly airsick so he didn't enjoy it much. In those days aircraft flew quite low and landed fairly frequently. They started their journey from the Lake Victoria port town of Kisumu and stopped at Khartoum on the and then to Cairo. In Cairo he met up with sister-in-law Jean Lankester and her husband, in those days Robin was teaching in Cairo.

Cairo was the supreme headquarters of all the troops in that area - the Middle East. From Cairo they flew on to London. It was a long night flight, straight back to England. By that time they had switched to a conventional airplane. He was given a bit of leave and General Platt let him go off and see Nancy and the family.

Then he went back to East Africa because it was decided that the East African Division was to be built up and moved to India and become part of the Far East forces under Earl Mountbatten, to try and recover Singapore.

He was put in charge of the main training camp near Nairobi to train reinforcements for his Division which was now in India and Burma. He was training troops for the King"s African Rifles (KAR), Kenya Regiment (KR) and Gunners. Eventually he was appointed to command the Anti-Tank Regiment and went off to India.

India. He flew to Cairo and from Cairo flew to India, arriving in Calcutta and then on to to Ranchi (Bihar) 200 miles north west of Calcutta - he didn't think he would ever get there. It was an old transport plane, with no seats, he lay amongst the sacks of mail and stuff. Thus the new commanding officer of the Anti-Tank Regiment arrived to take over his command.

By that time the antitank guns (16 pounders) were all mechanized. They were actually called the Golf Bag Regiment because they had anti-tank guns as their main artillery weapon but they were also armed with mortar because in the dense jungles of south east Asia they were unlikely to encounter many tanks, but they would be required if there was a break out, whereas if they were armed with mortars they could be quite useful, providing a concentration of mortars that was not normal for the infantry. The plan was to break out from the Japanese/Burma front and drive the Japanese back. This never happened because by the time they had completed training and were ready to move, the Atom Bombs had been dropped on Japan and the Japanese surrendered.

The bombing of Japan did not mean a lot at the time, they were just thankful the War was at an end. The War in Europe had ended in 1945. He never saw any fighting. The East African Division that had been withdrawn from the Japanese front and was reforming. They were training to go back and carry on the momentum of the battle, but they never got there. After that it was just a matter of getting the troops back to East Africa, sorting them out and sending them home, and getting home himself.

Colonel George Grimshaw, Battalion commander

They had a whole Division comprising 10,000 troops. The soldiers were from Kenya, Nyassaland, Uganda and Tanganyika. During this period the main thing was to keep them occupied and out of mischief whilst they were waiting for shipment to take them back to East Africa. They eventually got back to East Africa and returned to their homes and villages. They didn't worry about civilian clothes, they were only too glad to be released to go home.

After George got his Regiment off his hands, he flew to Cairo and then onwards to England. It was late 1946 when he got back and then he was posted to some "hopeless" place up in Yorkshire to take over a disbanded Anti-Aircraft Regiment and its stores and assets, which he refused to do simply because when he got there he asked where the ledgers and records were. He was not prepared to take over an Anti-Aircraft Regiment without a fully recorded inventory because he knew the sort of thing that could happen, he could be landed with absent material which he would have been charged for. He said that he would not take over unless he had it all on paper and could see the stores he was taking over. His stand at that point probably raised his status a bit and he was posted as Staff Captain of the School of Artillery at Larkhill. He moved down there and was at the headquarters there for a couple of years.

For his performance during the early part of the War George was made (December 1941) a Member of the British Empire (MBE), and received three "mentioned in dispatches"\

Garth - an interlude - 1944– 1946

During the latter part of the war he moved Nancy from Levels Dean back to Garth, where she could look after herself, as he thought it was time she stood on her own feet, John was born there on July 12th 1945.

Nancy's neighbours at Garth were the Shepherds - Ernie Shepherd. Mrs. Shepherd was a nurse actually and she more or less delivered John when the time came.

The first time that Nancy had to manage a home on her own was at Garth. She had maid/cook and a gardener who was fired after he was found stealing. George returned in 1946 to really get to know his three children. Garth was rather different to Levyls Dene. There were frequent walks, via Halfpenny Lane, to nearby St Martha's for Sunday church services and to put bunches of violet on Violet's grave. Blackberry picking was always a popular pastime in September. Richard went to a school, Greenacres, on Long Down Road – he didn't like it much. Other interesting past times were walking the back paths to Guildford arriving on the High Street via Guildford Castle, and camping in a tent in the garden with Gink Lankester's (Robin's brother) two daughters, Pru and Madelaine (Madelaine was Gillian's age). Of course there were still visits to Levyls Dene, walking across the Downs, past the German prisoner of war camp, and though a back gate to Levyls Dene. At the time George would go daily to the War Office in London before his posting to Larkhill. Strangely Garth was really never imprinted in any ones mind as "home".

George - Between careers

George sold Garth, and then first rented a house at Shrewton on Salisbury Plains, not far from Larkhill. That winter 1946 was bitterly cold, very little heating (Britain was in its post war extremis – severe rationing under the austere Sir Stafford Cripps). George then bought Highfield in Shrewton. He knew a very nice Polish chap who had been in his Regiment who was a builder, and who replastered the old house that had been damaged during the War. They were there two years there. It was fun. A nice garden, horses, and a garden great for games like "kick the can", "beckoning" and "hide and seek". That was when they had there first taste of Coca Cola courtesy of an American Army officer, along with chocolate and other unavailable delights. Richard started going as a border to Cottesmore School in Sussex. Cottesmore was owned by George's boyhood friend, Michael Rogerson. It was a big change for Richard, far from home surrounded by what seemed hundreds of other small boys, In those days school fees were £60 per term.

George was appointed Q officer responsible for all the administration, buildings and design and construction of new buildings. It was very interesting and important as the work laid the foundation for the future School of Artillery. It had been started and the Officers' Mess had been built, but the rest of it was still very temporary. Whilst at Highfield third son Christopher was born in a nursing home in Salisbury on October 9th 1947.

He used to shoot rabbits all over Salisbury Plain. They would go out at night and have ragged beats in various places, they were shooting more than riding actually, but they had horses there.

It was whilst he was at Larkhill that he started sailing again. He bought Betsy, a yawl, and spent as much time as he could on her. The boat was anchored at Fawley (now a large refinery), a creek off Southampton Water. He jointly owned her with another officer in the Gunners who lived in Shrewton, but who didn't use the boat very much, George used it most of the time. He just sailed on the Solent. They had small children on board all the time. Gillian had her friend Jill Fox, who now lives over the other side of Tavistock. Nancy quite enjoyed it, John was a youngster then, they hadn't take Chris, who was tiny, and was left behind on those occasions. Richard was a bit of a dare devil on the boat. It was quite a big boat - they did have one exciting incident. They were sailing one day back from the Isle of Wight to Southampton and suddenly spotted a canvas canoe, mostly submerged, in the middle of the Solent, so they heaved it on board and when and handed it over to the Customs. The latter advertised it, it wasn't claimed and George paid ten shillings for it. That was their first sort of auxiliary boat; but Betsy was a lovely boat. Betsy was a yawl; she had a canoe stem and was built specially really for the East Coast. The person who had had her before was a very well known Gunner sailor and he was getting a bigger boat, or a better boat. Sailing Yacht Clubs in England acquired German boats and he probably got one of those. They used to go off for the week-end on Betsy and go over to the Isle of Wight and camp the other side and sail around. Very low key sailing, they never did any ambitious sailing on her. Gillian had a pony at Highfield. She and Richard used to ride the pony.

While George was in Kenya during the war he took part in the Officers' Christian Union. He had visited quite a lot of the Church Missionary Society (CMS) mission stations, when he had had days off. It was at that time that he met Howard Church. For some reason or another the Secretary of the Mission in Kenya had written home (George had carried a lot of papers home for them, got them through the censor, to CMS headquarters, which helped them quite a lot because otherwise it took ages to get letters back) suggesting that it would be a very good thing if George could come back to Kenya and join the CMS in some way. Max Warren CMS's Home Secretary had the idea of a Regional Secretary for Eastern Africa and contacted George about the job. George decided he had served his country well and for long enough. He retired from the Army in 1948 at the age of 38 and after - a 19 year army career, joined CMS, and went off to East Africa.

Sailing the yawl Betsy on the Solent - 1947

George Grimshaw - the Missionary

Uganda. In 1948 the family took the old unconverted troop ship S.S. Orbita from Liverpool and travelled to East Africa. On board families were segregated. It was very austere and basic. Men in separate communal cabins; the women and children in other "dorms". It was quite a trip, following the old sea route to India, via the Suez canal. After Aden, though, the ship turned south to Mombasa.

George's job was being "invented", nobody really knew what it involved. At that time there was a possibility of an East African Federation, and that the East African countries, Tanganyika, Kenya, Rwanda, Uganda and possibly Southern Sudan might well become a new political unit. To match these possible political changes CMS thought it might be a good thing to have a coordinated administration of some sort for the Missions instead of having separate missions in each country. However as soon as George arrived (1948) he realised that East Africa countries had no interest in a Federation of any sort. So any link between political ambitions and the Mission was just not realistic.

He was out there and nobody seemed to know what he was supposed to be doing – for that matter neither did he! However having been headquartered in East Africa during the War he knew all the countries much better than most people, because he had been in the War and none of the missionaries had. The missions were very parochial. In the beginning he used to wander round and just get in touch with them and meet the Bishops and be friends with some. He was first stationed in Uganda. The family lived on Namirembi Hill (Kampala's great cathedral hill - one of the Kampala's seven hills overlooking the city), in the Archdeacon's house. Bishop Stewart of Uganda saw him as a rival and didn't want him at all. The Bishop eventually sent him off to Kenya, a move that turned out for the good. Patsy was born at Namirembe on December 15 1949. She was born while George was up in Sudan. Patsy nearly didn't survive. In the hospital the custom was for the matron to come and visit anyone and kiss the very ill, her kiss of death!. Patsy got the kiss but thankfully lived!

Uganda was the lead mission in those days, and the Bishop of Uganda had a sort of aura round him of magnificence, power and history. A former Bishop of Uganda, Bishop Hannington had been murdered on the order of the King Mwanga II.

When George arrived in Uganda there was an ongoing "revival" - "Revival" meant the freeing itself from the Church, so it was a cause of contention between Bishop Stewart, who thought it was dangerous, and the Rwanda Mission where it originated. It was obvious at that time it had been very successful in weaning people from crime, and crowds of people came in from Rwanda and it was spreading to Uganda. George took a fairly neutral attitude, because he had to work with the pro-revival and the anti-revival people,

George was quite prepared to back the Bishop up in his work if he wanted him to. However the Bishop didn't want any other ideas, he was quite happy with his own views; and then, to complicate it further, Mary, his wife, who was a very well educated woman, and who was in with the university and educational people, was leading the women, who were beginning to cause "trouble" in the church. The Bishop didn't want another trouble-maker around. So when Max Warren, CMS Home Secretary in London, came out to visit it was decided that it was best for George to go off to Kenya. He had been in Uganda for 18 months.

During those 18 months in Uganda Gillian and Richard were at boarding schools (Nairobi Primary School and Limuru Girls School) in Kenya (they took an overnight train from Kampala to Nairobi). John and Chris were too young to be at school. Jacqueline Silcock was George's secretary in those days and was a good companion for Nancy when he was away. Marney, Richard's godmother, brought John and Chris out from England. She had been looking after the two young boys at Levyls Dene when George, Nancy, Gillian and Richard first went to Uganda. Both boys arrived with whooping cough. John had a terrible, terrible time, George thought he might die.

Kenya. George was a Humber fan, and he had Humber build him a special box body (station wagon) vehicle that was good for safari work. There was plenty of room for the whole family and a good load too. On leaving Uganda he drove the family down to Nairobi, where they initially stayed in the CMS guest house that in those days was on the edge (now virtually the city center!) of the town by the railway. The children were always getting in people's way! The only accommodation the Kenya Mission had for the family was a completely broken down mud house at Kabete (6 miles north of Nairobi) that was unsatisfactory from any point of view, but certainly for Nancy, because she was going to be left alone and would be very isolated on the edge of the Kikuyu country. So they became permanent residents of the guest house, until they heard of a doctor who was leaving for Canada, and who had a very nice house out at Karen on Windy Ridge, not far from the Karen Blixen's house and the Ngong Hills, that they came to love so much.

Windy Ridge. George bought it – selling his house in England - for about £4,000 (There wasn't any money from CMS to buy a house although, George discovered after he returned to England that the whole time he was at Karen the Bishop thought the CMS had bought the house and put it at George's disposal, and the other missionaries bore him a grudge because he had a better house than they). It was a very nice bungalow with about 10 acres of land. They moved there in 1949. By 1951 Richard was at the Prince of Wales School, John was at Nairobi Primary School, and Gillian at Limuru Girls School – all were boarders. Patsy was too young to go anywhere to begin with.

Nancy made the house into a sort of holiday home for missionaries who came down to Nairobi and stayed there longer than they wanted to stay in the CMS guest house.

They had very nice neighbours, especially Harold and Joyce Gardner. In 1949 Harold Gardner was just retiring as the Conservator of Forests and was a great gardener. They had quite a big family - two daughters and three sons. So it was very convenient because it was right for Nancy, particularly as George traveled so much. George's office was in Nairobi in a new office building, Church House, built by the Diocese, not far from the main Railway Station.

There was another very nice family, the Sherwoods, at the end of Windy Ridge, (the road that the houses were built along), who became great friends. So Nancy had good neighbours to support her in George's frequent absences - the Wilkinsons, next door were another nice family but were Roman Catholics!. There was a young lad, Alan Root, who lived with his mother just down the road, he kept snakes and had them all on edge (Alan is now a well know wildlife photographer, his father Harold Root, at an old age, worked as a consultant for Richard in the 1970s). They had a cook – Jose, and a faithful Christian house servant Geradi, and William, the gardener, who looked after the cows. George eventually got hold of some cows and set up a little small holding, he thought they ought to do something like that. One cross bred Jersey cow who was called mojo (Swahili for one) had only one teat, but she gave a lot of milk. They had bees for a short time too, until the bees were destroyed by army ants. They settled down well, Nancy had these nice neighbours and George was able to go off on extended safaris feeling comfortable that she was well looked after, even during the subsequent Mau Mau insurgency.

Down town Nairobi was about 10 miles from Karen, quite a little run in the car. Nancy's father died (1951) very soon after she got there; he was hit by a car whilst walking to Guildford, he died, but he left Nancy a bit of money with which she bought a car - a light green Ford Prefect - so she was able to get around with the family; life for the family was rather more settled there than it was in Uganda.

There was a Diocesesan complex including houses and a CMS Mission office not far from Nairobi Cathedral. William Carey was the Secretary at the time. George was given a couple of rooms and an office there. His secretary, Elizabeth Swayne, was a very fashionable American widow who initially lived with the family on Windy Ridge. Nancy had company, which was good, apart from having Patsy around the whole time. Elizabeth eventually married an eye doctor and lived a couple of hundred yards from the Grimshaws on Windy Ridge.

Nancy's mother, who was newly widowed, came to stay with them for a few months. She had traveled a lot before, and had been to Palestine; she wrote a very good diary about the trip that the family still has. (George saved it from destruction, when Jean and Nancy were sweeping everything into the dust bin after she died!). She was good company for Nancy. It was a big adjustment for her, not being used to the heat. George remembers having gone down to Mombasa to fetch her from the boat; driving back she was so hot that he made her undress herself, taking off all her winter woollies and stiff corset!

The Mau Mau insurrection started in 1952. Of course everybody's lives were effected to some degree or other. None of the CMS missionaries were armed in any sense, so they were no catch for the Mau Mau who often attacked to get weapons, There were only 27 Europeans altogether killed and they were, in nearly every case, killed for their weapons. One or two of them, who were very influential with the local Africans, were murdered, but they were separate from the missions. Richard recalls that during the emergency when he was at school the Prince of Wales School (now the Nairobi School) at Kabete that there were a few extra restrictions and the boarding houses (he was in Grigg) were surrounded with barbed wire fences and watch towers (more to keep the boys in than the terrorists out!). Military helicopters used to land on the playing fields in front of the school to deliver wounded soldiiers to the nearby military hospital. Mau Mau activities did restrict some of the visits to favourite fishing streams.

At Windy Ridge, George laid a very good "Murram" - laterite - hard tennis court, There were many fine games of tennis there. There was also a large shipping container that was converted into a pigeon house. There were hundreds of pigeons. the original brood came from Archdeacon Archibald Shaw - known affectionately as the "Arch". He was a retired

CMS missionary living in Karen. He had worked for years in the southern Sudan with the Dinka people whom loved him much. In his retirement he brought a number of Dinka's with him to Kenya. His faithful servant, Philip, was a grand young man. During the time George was in Uganda and Richard was at the Nairobi Primary School the "Arch" became a sort of surrogate father. Richard remembers the great teas that the Arch would provide, and the fun of shooting mouse birds in the grounds.

Life was simple in those Karen days. There always seemed a lot to do, a favourite was the walk to Dr. and Mrs. Patterson's house that took us through a beautiful forest with gorgeous swallow tail butterflies. At the end of the drive was another world. Dr. P was very old fashioned walking around in "plus-fours", his wife was German, and they lived in a lovely, but dark house, over looking the Ngong Hills. There son Daniel was a family friend, and of course the main attraction was the swimming pool. Sometimes the walk took them down the hill to Karen (Indian owned) stores (duka) where Nancy would buy bread and meat (boys meat for the servants and dogs meat - bones - for the dogs! Nobody bought special pet food in those days. The family was really quite self sufficient in food - milk, butter, vegetables, rabbit, chicken and eggs. Nancy kept very careful household accounts, recording every cent that she spent. Initially they had two Spaniels, Goldie and Blackie, both died suddenly (after a picnic on the Ngong Hills where they ate some strychnine baited meat). Then there was a black labrador called Trusty, a good family dog that everybody loved.

The boys were always tinkering with the two wheeled tractors that were used for ploughing. They were heavy and difficult to start. That is probably where all three of them became handy with their hands. Occasionally the family would visit Nairobi for clothes shopping, the occasional movie and church services at Nairobi Cathedral. George and Nancy were very instrumental in having a new church, St Francis, built at Karen. Before that, the Karen church was an old army hut not farm from their house on a very wet and muddy (black cotton) bit of land.

Mission Administration George traveled a lot meeting and helping mission staff. In the Upper Nile Diocese Bishop Wilson was very good, he took George round with him on some of his safaris and therefore got more recruits for his particular mission.

He had no written instructions or guidance as to what he was supposed to be doing, and no-one in East Africa really knew either, extraordinary really when one looks back at those days. George was really a mission administrator at large! It was all rather experimental, but the one thing he felt was important was, and it was clearly meant as his title was Regional Secretary for Kenya, Uganda and Sudan, was to get the missions to become more of a family. They were very isolated because of communication in those days and distances. Also they were traditionally very independent, because one had to be independent to start a mission. Often they were not all that friendly, as one missionary said, "that mission would never have started if those two missionaries hadn't quarreled". One of the two just got on his motorbike and drove off into the bush and started a new mission. George went round trying to find out their problems and where they were successful and where they were not, and how things were being built up, and then feeding the information back to other missions, all the time trying to encourage them to be interested in their fellow missionaries over the border. It sounds simple enough but they just weren't interested. They were so absorbed in their own problems and, of course, in those days there were many of them. Sometimes a woman missionary would be a schoolteacher in a mission 40 or 50 miles away from any other European. One of the things he tried to do was to encourage the CMS headquarters policy of not having missionaries by themselves, but linking them up.

He took Nancy round once or twice, up to the Sudan for her to see what was going on, so that when the missionaries came to stay with at Windy Ridge she would have a better feeling of where they had come from. One of Nancy's great assets was that she could give them a comfortable home in a lovely situation and spoil them a bit. A favourite pass time was to take the visitors around the game parks. On one occasion they had the whole of the Uganda Girls' Netball Team staying with them, they slept on the floor in one room, and were so excited to have a hot shower. They were great fun. So Nancy had a part to play as well.

The Bishops were all CMS and they were accountable, in a sense, in their ordinary straightforward administration to the Mission Secretary. Each diocese had its own Mission Secretary. George displaced them gradually, until he had overall control.

He tried to reduce friction between he and the missionaries. He tried to keep a low profile. He didn't bother them very much as long as they were happy doing what they wanted and were happy with the Secretary and how he handled them. When the Mission Secretary retired he took over. Gradually he built up a regional office, at the same time it was quite clear that the mission aspect had to give way to the diocesan aspect, so over time a lot of the work that the Mission Secretary had done, as well as the relationship between the missionaries and the local church, changed and to become eventually as they are now, partners in the church.

The whole of that period was trying to let the situation in the local church develop more and more. He was there for the first appointment of African Bishops, for instance. He arranged a very big service, they all came, from Sudan and Uganda and Upper Nile, and at the same time had Assistant Bishops appointed and consecrated. Eventually of course most of the Africans took over from the English Bishops. When he went back to England on one of his earlier furloughs he remembers talking to the Home Secretary (Max Warren) in London, and he realized that it was quite a new idea to them that there should be an independent church there; they hadn't thought of that, that the church would become independent and could have its own mission, diocese and committees.

George's friend John Taylor, who was one of the great heroes and icons of the CMS Missionary world, who has been greatly honoured as Principal of the Theological College in Uganda, George was staying with him very early on, and of course having been in the Army and seen what Africans could do. George had a fairly revolutionary approach to Africans, compared to most others who still looked upon them as being mission boys. Later John Taylor told him *"you know one of the first things you said to me was - when are you going to be replaced by an African?"*

Africanisation was on its way. In Nairobi he was in touch with a lot of the more politicized Africans. He used to have lunch quite often with Tom Mboya (one of the great hopes of a new Kenya, who was sadly assassinated after independence). He used to come into the canteen at Church House and George quite often had meals with him, and he recalled that on one of his safaris he stayed with some white Christian farmers at Kitale on the way to Uganda, and told them that he often dined with Tom Mboya who, of course, was anathema to farmers. *'What, with that man, you don't mean to say you consort with him do you?'* That was the sort of attitude in the early 1950s, but it all changed gradually.

The church was moving ahead, modernising and becoming independent faster than the government or the administration because it was unable to afford to recruit the numbers needed. George recruited teachers for the schools, as well as doctors and nurses, but had to get Government help to pay for them. Thus the stage was set that to replace the expatriate clergy and administrators with Africans. George was able to build up good relationships with the incoming African clergy and staff because they really wanted assistance – rather different from the expatriate mission staff. In retrospect he found it more worthwhile than he thought at the time, Even so there was a lot of opposition - The Bishops weren't by any means happy with his views and actions. The CMS Headquarters in London was in the vanguard of advance for Africans, whereas out in East Africa everybody was saying *'it's too soon'*.

The missionaries were gradually becoming less in numbers as the Africans were taking over, instead of having a lady missionary as headmistress of the local school, one would have an African man probably taking over as headmaster. More often they were paid for by government. The whole process was gradual, but still the church remained under the English bishops, who were under Lambeth, and thus was very much part of the Anglican Church. However there was a movement to Africanise the church. George remembers after being back in England for 12 years he went to the CMS headquarters in London and met Archbishop Suebi, who had become Archbishop of Uganda. When he first knew him he had just been ordained in Ruwanda.

Having been in the Army and seen Africans being given very important positions George realised they could be trained to take on pretty well anything as long as one trained them, and as long as one didn't ask them to take on too much, that was the danger, to ask them to do more than they could cope with. It seemed perfectly obvious to him that there were plenty of Africans who were capable of leading their own people in their spiritual lives. They were leading them and had been for years. Nearly all the early African headmasters of bush schools, may well have been the only Christian there and they would teach the Bible, or what they knew of it, in that bush school. Gradually they got trained and so there was a development of the Church.

It was not always easy for new African clergy. They were still many animists who believed in the spirits, and ancestral worship. George remembers going into one village in Northern Uganda and having a chat with the head man there and walked into the middle of the village and there was a stone there where their ancestors spirits dwelt and people would bring food and put it there and it disappears. The head man was a bit cynical about it, he knew what was going on, but a lot of the locals believed that their ancestors had come and taken the food. The clergy still believed in spirits and they had their witch doctors and they had their good witch doctors and their bad witch doctors.

At Namirembi, the Kabaka – the King of Buganda - was the great spiritual leader of the people. He had a great African hut, that was the original king's throne room, and had become the spiritual centre of the tribal believers and they thought that was the centre of their faith, rather like a Cathedral, but that faded after a bit as more and more people became Christians and understood more about Christianity and what it meant and who God was and so on and their tribal ancestral worship gradually faded out but not completely

George continued his mission of helping and intervening where he thought best. One such example was of a Leper Centre in the Upper Nile Diocese - in those days they were just beginning to cure leprosy involving very heavily handicapped patients, and it struck him straight away that the one thing they badly needed was a physio and occupational therapist. He was able to recruit these technicians – even though they had no particular religious affinity.

Another thing that caused a bit of a kafuffle at the time when he first went out was a CMS policy of making available more comforts for the missionaries. When he went up to the Sudan there was only one fridge in the whole mission. It belonged to the Mission Secretary's because he had independent means and was fairly rich. He and his wife had no children, and had a fridge. George caused a bit of a rumpus because the other missionaries said *'oh we don't have fridges, we don't have this, that and the other'*; and George said *'the CMS is offering this to you and it will make your life easier if you have a fridge and a few other necessities"* and it was hardly believable but it was a real battle to get them to accept the idea of having more comforts. Part of their calling was to be uncomfortable, it was part of their spirituality and they had to learn to accept and gradually use them.

Family holidays in Kenya were always fun. Two or three Christmas holidays were spent on the Kenya coast at a lovely beach, Tiwi, south of Mombasa. The family loved Tiwi with its lovely long white beaches and protected water between the edge of the reef and the beach. George used to rent fishing huts up on some of the Mt. Kenya streams where he and the older children would fish for rainbow trout. One holidays the whole family drove to Ruwanda, staying with Joe Church and his famly at Gisenye. The family frequently had picnics on the Ngong Hills, it was a place to walk freely, with wonderful views of the great Rift Valley to the west. On clear days one could see Mt. Kenya, the Aberdare Mountains and Mt. Kilamanjaro from the top of those hills.

Another occasion George, Gillian and Richard, together with Gillian's friend from Limuru School and her 65 year old mother, Mrs. Taylor, who farmed coffee at Arusha, climbed Mount

Tiwi Beach near Mombasa, Kenya. 1954, left to right: Gillian, Richard, Nancy with Patsy, John, Chris and George.

Kilimanjaro - four days up (from Moshi) and two days down. It was quite an event. In those days (1954) not many people climbed the mountain. One had to book the three huts, one at 9,000 ft just at the top of the forest zone, another on the moorlands between Kibo and Mawenzi at 11,000 ft in the moorland zone, and the top hut at 14,000 ft at the foot of Kibo at the bottom of the scree. Richard recalls that it was quite an easy walk up to the top hut, of course they had porters to carry the supplies. From the top hut to the crater of Kibo it was hard work on a steep scree slope. George, Gillian and her friend got dreadful mountain sickness and could not go beyond the Top Hut. Richard and old Mrs. Taylor made it to Gilman's Point (18,330 ft). It was bitterly cold up there with fabulous views. In those days there were very few climbers on the mountain, and they were the only climbing team there at the time. Two years later Richard climbed the mountain from Rongai (Kenya side) - three days to the top - 15,000 ft altitude change - no wonder climbers suffered from mountain sickness. In those days looking there was a lot more snow and glaciers on the mountain than there is today; also the forests on Kilimanjaro and Mt Elgon have been severely decimated.

Another year the family was in Uganda on holiday - visiting the Murchison Falls on the River Nile, where the river pours through a 20 ft gap. In those days the park was full of wildlife, elephant, hippo, crocodile, buffalo etc. On the way back they climbed Mt. Elgon, an 11,000 ft volcano that straddles the Uganda/Kenya border. It was just a days walk ending on a coffee farm near Kitale.

George learnt Swahili, but not fluently – unfortunately none of his family had any language ability!

He had met many of the missionaries during the War because his Army responsibilities took him all round East Africa to check the quality and the recruitment of Africans for the East African Army. It was during those days that he met Howard and Lizo Church – they became life long friends - at their mission station at Chagoria on the foothills of Mt. Kenya. He used to go to them quite often. They were on a route round Mount Kenya to the Northern Frontier district. He met a lot of missionaries there, as a Christian, he used to deliberately go and meet them, and cheer them on their way.

In those days there were few places to stay and the general practice was to stay with the missionaries, they all had quite big houses and there was plenty of room. George could drop in, they had what was called a Merrick rate, 7 shillings a day – bed and board.

Nancy would never have sent the children to school in England. It was either altogether in Kenya or altogether back in England. Most people thought the Grimshaws would stay in Kenya forever. The Gardners for instance, the great neighbours across the road, were quite upset when told that they were leaving. They might well have been there for life. But because of schooling and education it was decided to go on furlough and decide during that time whether to return or not. George was given the opportunity of taking on a job at CMS headquarters to look after their overseas visitors. After much debate and recognition that George had completed the regionalization task that he went to Africa for it was agreed that he would return to England. So instead of Nancy and the children going back with him he went back at the end of the furlough on his own for 6 months. He was out there on my own, just clearing up and waiting to go back and take up this job when it was available. Nancy was never able to say farewell to her friends, so for her it was an abrupt change.

George decided that they had to come back to England because the children were all at various colleges and schools. John and Christopher needed a better school than they could get in Kenya. They let the house in Kenya, and later Richard, who went to Kenya with the World Bank, sold it.

During their furlough in 1959, they were able to buy Nightingale Old Farm, at Woodstreet Green, close to Guildford. They borrowed the money from the bank to buy Nightingale Old Farm, but as they were old bank customers, there was no difficulty about that. It was the National Provincial Bank in Guildford.

England Again - Nightingale Old Farm (NOF)

Like his mother, Violet, George had a good eye for property. Nightingale Old Farm, known to all as NOF, was just a couple of miles down the road from Nancy's brother Douggie's home. NOF, located on 2 acres adjacent to the village green at Woodstreet (5 miles west of Guildford, and just north at the bottom of the Hog's Back), was a Queen Anne period house that nobody wanted to buy because it was damp. Dad discovered that the ancient slate damp course was 18 inches below the soil surface. So he got the place cheap, and with the help of his sons proceeded to dig out the soil on two sides of the house to below the damp course. That did the trick and the house dried out.

It was a great family home, and soon the main lawn was turned into a grass tennis court, with raspberry netting strung up on poles to keep the balls in. They got rid of most of the moss, and then settled down to many years of glorious tennis parties that went late into the long summer evenings. At the other end of the village, next to the pub, was John and Rosemary Bristowe (Rosemary was Douggie's daughter). Richard and John worked on the neglected village green, and soon there was a quite respectable cricket "square" and outfield. That was the start of Woodstreet Green village cricket - still continuing today. Bristowes moved and Granny Gilliat bought the house

NOF tennis four, George, Duggie Gilliat, Robin Lankester, and Pat Gilliat

and moved in. Next to come was Tommy's widow Joan Grimshaw - she bought the "old smithy" and lived there until she died in 2006 at the age of 98. Thus there was quite a family gathering. Rosemary's brother Michael Gilliat and his wife Jill lived quite close, and both he and John Bristowe were frequent tennis party guests.

As a family, they had great fun at NOF. George kept everybody busy tending the big garden. There was always wood and grass to cut, lawns to weed, fruit to pick, and paths to lay. George never had a new car. At NOF he had an old prewar Austin - with a slipping clutch - and a gear box that was not synchronized; so to change gear one had to double-de-clutch. It leaked oil dreadfully.

George and Nancy's 25th wedding anniversary (1962) at NOF. Cutting the cake in the kitchen.

In NOF days Richard was at Wye College, having a good time, and getting a degree in Agricuture, John and Chris were at Hazelgrove School in Somerset (Robin Lankester was headmaster, ably helped by his wife Jean - Nancy's younger sister), after which they went to Monkton Combe School near Bath, Patsy went to Tormead in Guildford. Gillian had graduated from Bristol University, married Harry Foot and headed off to Nyasaland (now Malawi) as a District Officer. In 1961 Richard went to Trinity College, Cambridge, followed by a year at the Imperial College of Tropical Agriculture in Trinidad, before being posted in 1964 as an Agricultural Officer in Northern Rhodesia soon to be Zambia. The family attended the church in Worplesdon and St. Alban's in Woodstreet Green.

George - A London job

Settled back in England George started commuting to London, which was a bit of a shock. His office was in the famous CMS headquarters at Salisbury Square just next to St Bride's church. In those days a lot of the overseas students were mainly ex mission school students - because most of the schools had been managed by the mission. The young students used to come to CMS for help, and the latter would try and make sure they had accommodation and got the courses they wanted to do and so on. CMS had to meet a lot of the adults who came too, like the clergy who were coming for courses in England or on attachment to parishes in England. George and his helpers would get them to second hand clothes shops to get them kitted out with warm clothes.

Most arrived in groups but sometimes one of the clergy would come by himself or just with his wife they would be met at Heathrow airport. As the numbers grew the more complex managing them became. It was a joint operation with the Church of England as well being funded by the CMS and the Church Commissioners.

He gradually got a team going, and he them to get together and meet, because an awful lot of them were very much alone. They created a Supper Club, attended by as many as 100 students sometimes. On some occasions students provided the meals or at least cooked them. George remembers getting a taxi once, down to Cable Street to pick up an old Nigerian lady who cooked the supper for everybody, and brought the supper back to CMS headquarters. Various volunteers organised the suppers, those were quite useful occasions because they got to know each other.

CMS sold the valuable Salisbury Square site and moved to a new headquarters in Waterloo Road. It was about then that

George got involved more with the national side of the work, as well as the CMS side and there was a regular meeting of all the overseas student organizing groups that he was a member of. He ended up being Chairman of the group for a short time. At that time he felt that accommodation for the students was so difficult that another hostel was needed. There were a number of hostels - the Baptists had a hostel and there was a central hostel for students. George persuaded the Church Commissioners and the CMS that they should try and get an Anglican hostel going and actually managed to get two going at the same time. A conference was held at Lee Abbey where it was decided to start a new hostel, they bought some houses up in the Kiddlington area and a row of adjacent houses in Sussex Gardens (near Paddington Satation) that had to be redesigned and rebuilt for students. Thus accommodation was arranged for about three to four hundred students.

At Sussex Gardens, Robin Lancashire (later to become Chaplain of Bath University) was the first warden. He took over and moved into Sussex Gardens. It was officially opened by the Duke of Edinburgh. George succeeded in getting Lord Marsh to be Chairman. Marsh was in touch with Robin Woods, who was the Dean of Windsor, and between them they got the Duke to come and open it

George raised money from various sources; the Bishop of London produced some money and various businesses, but basically it was funded by the local council because they wanted accommodation and they were only too glad for somebody to buy up some of these old dilapidated, run-down, buildings and convert them into something that could be used. It worked for a time but eventually petered out because it was very difficult to create the revenue needed to operate it. Costs were going up and the British Council wouldn't support a fee increase for the students, and so the hostel began getting into debt, and Robin Woods, who was Chairman of the committee at that time decided, quite rightly, that the Church wasn't sufficiently interested in running a hostel. It was closed down and sold.

George's nephew (Tommy's son), now Sir Nicholas Grimshaw

K.B.E. – a well know London architect and President of the Royal Academy – was hired as a young man to create the design for Sussex Gardens. It took about 18 months to get undertake the renovations and it operated for about 5 or 6 years. The building is still standing and has been converted into flats. The whole venture was rather short term filling a gap that was badly needed at the time. George was involved for ten years by the time the overseas groups had their own organisations going or were providing their own accommodation.

Michelpaige Farm in Sussex was another effort to get a suitable place for students to get together, interact and get to know each other. Michaelpaige is owned by St Hilda's community. The community was winding up and there was no future for it. At that time George happened to attend a conference at Rugby where he met a Dr. Gibson, who had been running the community, and he didn't know what to do with it. Gibson suggested to George that it might be good for overseas students to give them an opportunity to get together and help them acclimatise to British surroundings and so on.

The community used to farm the land and also there was a school across the road - the school and the farm eventually became independent, but the farm house, the barn and the chapel was retained by the community. Michelpaige nowadays is more generally used by local parishes as a place where people can go and meet. CMS never had any resident there, there was a discussion about it as to whether they should have a caretaker, but never did; the students went there for weekends and were expected to leave it in good order for the next lot. It worked pretty well really.

During this period Nancy was at home, there were always people staying at Nightingale Old Farm. George brought them down and Nancy looked after them. It was during this time that Boyago Ademolo became part of the family. His father was Chief Justice of Eastern Nigeria, later Nigerian High Commissioner in London, and finally Chief Justice of Nigeria, and was a very keen CMS supporter. The Chief Justice was looking for somewhere for his son to stay when he came to school at Wellingborough. Boyago regularly came for holidays and half-terms etc.

The Overseas Students' Commendation Centre was the central organisation that people concerned with overseas students joined. George was Acting Chairman for a time and went over to America with a group to link up their work with overseas students. The Americans had an organisation that dealt with overseas students. There they learned that British students were overseas students in America! On his first visit he went to see some overseas students in one of the universities and they were all British! There were all sorts of organisations and charities that had been set up to look after overseas students. Eventually there was a Commission, as there always is in the Church, to review the CMS and the work that the CMS and the Church were doing. It was decided that it wasn't the sort of work the church should be doing.

George knew a lot of people and many more knew him, even if he didn't know them. On one occasion a man came into his office and said '*I know you. You probably don't know me but I know you, I recognised your signature as soon as I saw it on your letter*' - he'd been a cashier in the bank in Nairobi! George used to invite some of the ex-missionaries and to join his staff, and had quite a team of about half a dozen or more people working at CMS House, including Hermionne Baker who looked after the many nurses who came over for training. When he came back to England he was dealing with all the overseas students, not just East Africans, however East and West Africans seemed to be the majority, but lots of Indians came too.

Eventually he retired in 1970 at the age of 60 and moved down to Devon. He didn't have to retire, but he did because the Commission had decided that the work was not what they wanted to go on with.

He was disappointed in a way because he liked dealing with the people themselves, the Commission didn't like that, they didn't want Summer Camps and activities that they would be responsible for, rather they wanted someone to go around the churches and tell them about the students and leave it at that.

He could have continued if he had wanted to, but he would have had to change his job, or change the way he did it. He decided it was time for other things that would reacquaint him with what he enjoyed in his youth.

Retirement - the Patriarch.

George retired when he was 60 (September 1970). To re-cap the family status at that time. Gill and Harry (Foot) were about to leave Malawi, they came back and bought NOF when George and Nancy moved to Devon. They had three children, Diana, David and Stephen. Richard married to Susan Bathurst-Brown was working for the World Bank as an agriculturist in Nairobi, they had three children, Carole, Nicola, and Shelagh. John, an engineer, was recently married to Rosalind and at the time had no children and were living in Bristol, and Chris, a veterinarian, and Patsy a school teacher were unmarried.

Stoke Gabriel, Devon. George and Nancy were keen to move to the west country. Nancy's sister, Jean and husband Robin Lankester lived near Bath, Brother Pat Gilliat and wife Noreen lived in Bath, and their close friends Howard and Lizzo Church lived on Dartmoor in Devon. Dad loved sailing, so they found Stoke Gabriel, a small village located on the north side of the River Dart, some 7 miles up stream from Dartmouth.

There they bought an old Georgian house with character, made the minimum renovations and moved in. The house was on a steep slope halfway up the village with a nice view towards the River Dart. There was no connection from the cellar to the ground floor so John and Chris dug through solid rock to create a passage and staircase to the main floor - quite a feat!.

On one of his trips to Devon George saw for sale a small day cruiser on a trailer on the side of the road. He bought it on the spot and called it Griffin. He now had a boat again and found a mooring at Duncannon, a short walk up river from Stoke Gabriel. He kept that mooring for many years, handing it over to Chris who keeps his boat there now. Then he wanted to do something with the village youth and he set up a "Learn to Sail" program using Optimists. Eventually they had about 12 Optis and it is said that he taught every child in the village how to sail, some of them went on to be regional and national sailors. He became Commodore of the Stoke Gabriel Sailing Association.

Whilst at Stoke Gabriel, son Chris who was the a veterinarian married Claire Davis of Sharpham Barton (near Totnes) and proceeded to produce four daughters - Julia, Joanna, Jenny, and Georgina. Patsy married Alec Fostiropoulis and had four children - Anna, Eleni, Michael and Mary. By this time John had three children Jem, Francis (Frank) and Ester. So George

George taught dinghy sailing at Stoke Gabriel and was Commodore of the Stoke Gabriel Sailing Association

and Nancy had by the mid 1980's 17 grandchildren, and one more in 1993 with the birth of Richard and Xiao Meng's daughter Lily, making 18 in all.

Ringmore In the early 1980's George and Nancy moved to an old house known as Middle Manor, in the village of Ringmore. He said he had to move there so as to force a parent to take over the Stoke Gabriel Sailing program! This remote village is only half a mile from the sea, a few miles west of Kingsbridge. The move was a new adventure. A small and close knit community that they soon became much involved with. George loved the old Norman church and was Church Warden for a number of years. He was also at one time Chairman of the village council, and Village Historian doing much to further the ancient history of the village - going back to the Doomsday Book.

In Ringmore George was able revert to his childhood passion relating to nature and conservation. He and others cut paths through "Badger Wood" on the west side of the valley so as to watch the badgers that lived there. He also purchased the neighboring barn with its lovely clock operated by great weights and which rang a bell every hour. They got used to that

George, Nancy, and devoted Busby at Ringmore (1980s).
View from garden to Aymer Cove

what ever the time of night! Additionally they bought a small wood at the end of the garden - of course new paths were built to access it. He loved the birds that lived in the garden. Hawks nested in the woods, pheasants ambled onto the lawn in front of the hose and the robins and tits befriended him until his death.

60th Wedding Anniversary November 30 1997 at Kingston Church

During their time in Devon the family house parties were revived again - using Chris's wonderful facilities and setting at Sharpham Barton. On such occasions the Grimshaws, Gilliats and Lankesters got together again to relive the house parties that were held in the late 50's and 60s at Hazelgrove House at Sparkford, Somerset, where Granny Gilliat presided as family matriarch. At Sharpham, George now the patriarch presided, and once again, tennis, boating,

Aymer Cove viewd from Nancy's favorite spot - Toby's Point

George (in his 80s) with son John

swimming, croquet, and endless discussion and debate was the form.

In 1998 George and Nancy celebrated their 60th wedding anniversary with a big family gathering. They lived a contented life with friends and family as frequent visitors, walks to Toby Point and the beach at Aymer Cove, the cliff walk, and walks

Family houseparty at Sharpham Barton - 1990

Patsy, Nancy, George, Chris, Gill, John, and Richard (1990) on Dartmoor. Visits to Sharpham to join Chris and Claire on the River Dart, and for many family house parties there. Sadly, in her eighties Nancy broke a leg and died shortly after in May 2000. George had a clock on the Ringmore Church tower installed in her memory.

George lived on for another eight years. He visited Richard, Xiao Meng (who Richard married in 1992), and Lily in the North West of the USA for his 90th birthday where once again he took the wheel of Moonshadow (Richard's sloop) and sailed the beautiful waters of Bellingham Bay.

On his return to England he settled back into Middle Manor becoming less mobile but still determined to be master of his life. For those last three years of he was cared for by the wonderful Lorallee and by his children

George, 2004, in his much loved garden at Middle Manor - still mobile

George, photographed by niece Tessa, in July 2008, just six weeks before he died

who visited him regularly and supported him. He refused to move from Middle Manor, and for his last year was bedridden in his bedroom from where he could still see the sea and the Eddystone Light (some 20 miles away in the English Channel), where the robins would fly through the window to see him, and where he held small tea parties for his village friends, and where he lived with his many memories.

George was a great letter writer and kept up with what was going on in the world. Naturally he had strong views - in one letter to Richard he wrote in 2007:

"Evidently in the 1770's Ringmore was more or less blown and flooded away by violent storms. In the next century we had 4 months without rain. The only water in the village was from the well behind my barn. Global warming is rubbish. There always has been pollution with extreme patches and always will be. After all we are now in the 4th Ice Age and must be getting near the top of the hot slope. In a few more 100's of years people will be calling for "global cooling". the young generation don't have to worry about GW - instead they have to worry about this scientific monster - computers that the scientific boys have created but cannot control!"

George had a love hate relationship with computers - he used to email his family and friends, and was proud of the fact that he could do so, but never understood how to "manage" the computer which at times sent him to distraction!.

He died on August 28th 2008, alert and in command until the end. He was buried on his 98th birthday in the Church yard - a great funeral for a great family man, a soldier and a gentleman - a man faithful to his Lord and his country until the very end.

Gone From My Sight
by Henry Van Dyke

I am standing upon the seashore. A ship, at my side, spreads her white sails to the moving breeze and starts for the blue ocean. She is an object of beauty and strength. I stand and watch her until, at length, she hangs like a speck of white cloud just where the sea and sky come to mingle with each other.
Then, someone at my side says, "There, she is gone"
Gone where?

Gone from my sight. That is all. She is just as large in mast, hull and spar as she was when she left my side.
And, she is just as able to bear her load of living freight to her destined port.

Her diminished size is in me -- not in her.
And, just at the moment when someone says, "There, she is gone,"
there are other eyes watching her coming, and other voices ready to take up the glad shout, "Here she comes!"

And that is dying...

Final Resting place for George and Nancy in an English country church yard at Ringmore

EPILOGUE

George and Nancy lived in Devon for more than 30 years and they very much loved the countryside that surrounded the Parish of Ringmore. They knew the woods, paths, buildings, trees, birds, sea, homes and people better than many of their fellow parishioners. The family wanted to leave an everlasting memorial to them, one that would still be visible in future millennia. John, the family path finder, came up with the idea of establishing weathered granite boulders (from the Lee Moor Quarry on Dartmoor) of considerable size at strategic locations where public footpaths crossed the parish boundary - see map. It was a community project with parishioners and family participating. Over a period of three days 18 enormous

Ringmore Parish Boundary Stone Walks

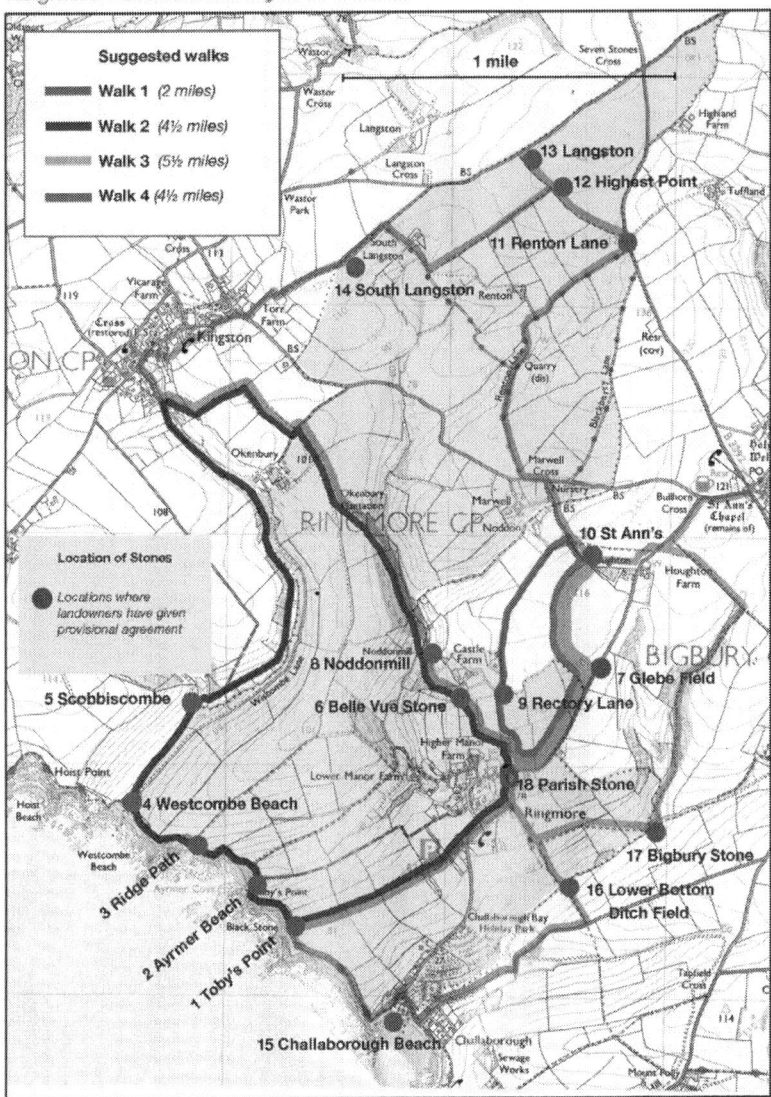

boulders (some weighing 5 tons or more were lifted from the quarry and trucked to the different boundary locations where they were maneuvered into position. Each was located with a view of the sea, or a stream or the rolling South Devon countryside. Each stone covered a time capsule depicting something typical of the present era. The master, or parish stone, was placed in the car park opposite the church. This stone has a plaque of dedication and a map of the stone locations.

Apart from the people of the Parish, George and Nancy's children, grandchildren and great grandchildren turned out in force to help and to dedicate the project at Ringmore Church on September 26th 2010. It was a great occasion with one last family picnic on the beach at Aymer Cove, followed by a service of dedication at the Church, and tea at the hall. What a memorial of remembrance!

The village stone pointing to Ringmore Church and the clock on the tower that George gave in memory of Nancy

A large rock being carried along one of Ringmore's narrow lanes

A rock brought from Dartmoor being placed on the beach at Challborough

John Grimshaw, the master planner of the Stones project, with the Aymer Cove stone.

Made in the USA
Lexington, KY
19 February 2018